LETTERKENNY INSTITUTE
OF TECHNOLOGY

THE ENGINEERING INDUSTRY OF THE NORTH OF IRELAND

W. E. COE MA, PhD

A publication of the Institute of Irish Studies
Queen's University, Belfast

DAVID & CHARLES: NEWTON ABBOT

MOBILE STORE

7153 4370 x

Printed in Great Britain by
Latimer Trend & Company Limited Plymouth
for David & Charles (Publishers) Limited
Newton Abbot Devon

Contents

6   *Contents*

List of Illustrations

PLATES

IN TEXT

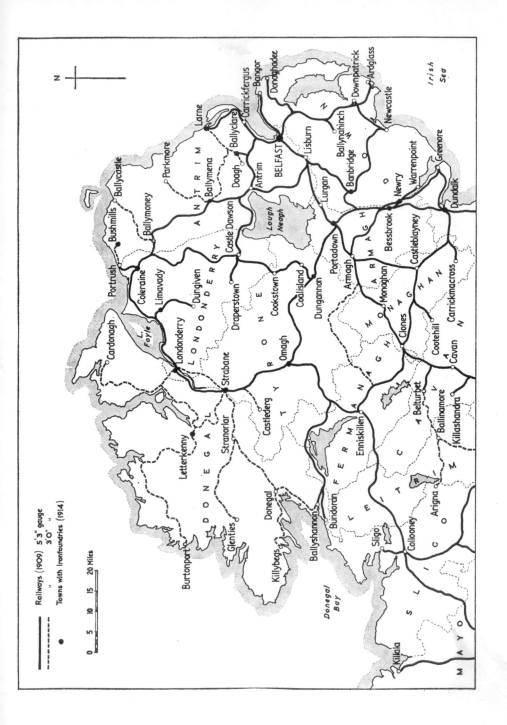

N

Irish Sea

Ardglass
Downpatrick
Donaghadee
Bangor
Newcastle
Carrickfergus
Larne
Greenore
Ballyclare
Warrenpoint
Ballynahinch
Doagh
Dundalk
Ballymena
Antrim
Lisburn
Newry
BELFAST
Lurgan
Banbridge
Parkmore
Castleblayney
Bessbrook
Ballycastle
Ballymoney
Portadown
Armagh
A R M A G H
Carrickmacross
Bushmills
Castle Dawson
Monaghan
A N T R I M
Lough Neagh
Clones
Portrush
Coleraine
Durgiven
Coalisland
M O N A G H A N
Cavan
Limavady
Drapestown
Cookstown
Dungannon
Cootehill
L O N D O N D E R R Y
Cardonagh
Omagh
Belturbet
Londonderry
T Y R O N E
Ballinamore
L. Foyle
Strabane
F E R M A N A G H
Killashandra
Letterkenny
Stranorlar
Castlederg
Enniskillen
L E I T R I M
Arigna
D O N E G A L
Bundoran
Burtonport
Donegal
Ballyshannon
Colloney
Sligo
Glenties
S L I G O
Killybegs
Donegal Bay
Killala
M A Y O

CHAPTER ONE

Introduction

ENGINEERING is not so much one industry as a family of industries. For practical purposes it may be regarded as the production of machinery, prime movers, mechanically propelled vehicles, implements and tools. The industry is commonly understood to include only engineering manufacturing, as the installation of equipment is often carried out by other industrial groups such as electrical contractors. Civil engineering is part of the construction industry, and shipbuilding is also distinct from the engineering industry, although it is closely allied with it. The various branches of the industry are united by the use of common metalworking techniques, the employment of similar grades of labour, and a well-established system of industrial relations.

In the north of Ireland, the growth of the engineering industry made possible the mechanisation of the linen industry. Iron and steel shipbuilding developed with the aid of techniques used in the boilermaking section of the engineering industry, and marine engineering later became a major activity of the local shipbuilders. Nevertheless, until recent years the north of Ireland was better known for linen and shipbuilding than for engineering. Since the war, linen and shipbuilding have contracted, while engineering has expanded until it is now the largest manufacturing industry in Northern Ireland, and the one which seems to have the greatest potential for future growth.

Since the north of Ireland has no useful resources of iron or coal, and at the beginning of the nineteenth century had few people with special skills in machinemaking or engineering management, it is surprising that an engineering industry developed in the area and even more so that some sections of the industry rapidly gained a foothold in the world market. What follows is an attempt to explain why the industry was established and why it assumed its present structure.

The area covered has more in common with the six counties of Northern Ireland than with the nine counties of the province of Ulster, but there are no tidy territorial limits. The self-employed metal craftsmen were spread throughout the countryside, and in the nineteenth century most provincial towns had ironfoundries which undertook the manufacture of some types of machinery, but for a long time large-scale engineering works were confined to Belfast. It was not until the middle of the present century that the engineering industry began to extend beyond the city into other parts of the north of Ireland.

CHAPTER TWO

Independent Craftsmen

THE groups of craftsmen who supplied the market for metal products and machinery before the industrial revolution, developed skills in metalworking and machine construction which made an important contribution to the development of the engineering industry.

Smiths

Up to the beginning of the nineteenth century, the smiths were the principal suppliers of tools, implements, and wrought-iron ware. In Ireland their market was limited by the general lack of prosperity, and their numbers declined throughout the century, most rapidly during and immediately after the potato famine of the late 1840s. By the beginning of the present century the majority of smiths were no longer self-employed, but were working in the shipyards and engineering works.

Most of the self-employed smiths were to be found in the countryside and the villages. The countryman's preference for traditional designs in implements, tools, and ironwork tended to protect the local smith from competition from Britain and elsewhere, but prejudice could operate as easily against local manufacturers as for them. In the early 1840s, reaping hooks made at Bushmills in county Antrim were sold in Scotland, England, and America, but not locally, for prejudice against home produce was strong in the minds of the peasantry.[1] So long as the horse continued to provide power for transport and agriculture, rural smiths were needed to shoe horses and repair horse-powered equipment. Their services were still much in demand in 1914, when there were some 100,000 farm horses in what is now Northern Ireland. There was no rapid decline in the horse population until after the second world war, but by the middle of the 1960s there were less than 4,000 farm horses left and only some 100 smiths engaged in horse shoeing, and for the great majority of them it was not a full-time occupation.[2] A hundred years before there had been more than 3,000 rural smiths in the same area.

The self-employed town smiths also depended for a living mainly on horse shoeing and repairs. There was little local demand for architectural wrought iron, for cast iron was available when the building industry expanded in the north of Ireland in the nineteenth century, and it was used where possible on account of its comparative cheapness. Only a few firms, most of them in Belfast, made wrought-iron products such as tools, safes, weighbridges and scales. The production of hardware might have appeared to be a profitable activity for smiths in the north of Ireland, for the high value of the finished product compared favourably with the cost of the raw materials, but by the end of the eighteenth century the English hardware makers were able to undersell the Irish smiths in their own market by reason of greater specialisation and better commercial organisation, as well as cheaper raw materials and fuel. With improvements in transport, the local market gradually came to be supplied from Britain and overseas.

Cutlery was never extensively made in Ireland, though in the middle of the nineteenth century there were makers of repute in Clonmel, Cork, and Dublin. In the 1840s, Richard Hurles of Enniskillen gained a wide reputation for his knives and razors, and became cutler to three or four royal families in Europe, but the business did not survive him.[3] By 1900, cutlery making had almost ceased throughout Ireland. Lack of traditional skills can, of course, be a positive advantage in certain circumstances, for when, in 1960, Oneida Silversmiths established a factory at Bangor, county Down, to produce cutlery by the most up-to-date methods, one of the attractions of the area was the absence of the Sheffield system of production by self-employed specialists in each stage of cutlery making. This method of organisation had proved adequate in the nineteenth century, but it prevented the cutlery industry speedily adopting modern production techniques.

Most of the Irish gunsmiths worked in Dublin or Cork, and in the north of Ireland only a score of gunsmiths can be traced who were in business at one time or another between 1750 and 1825. By the middle of the nineteenth century the 'gunsmiths' of the provincial towns had nearly all become mere dealers or gun repairers. Belfast had one important gunmaking firm, Joseph Braddell & Son of Castle Place, established in 1811. They made shotguns, rifles, pistols, and airguns, and in 1893 they claimed to be the largest gun manufacturers in Ireland, specialising in shotguns and 'Ulster Bull-dog' revolvers.[4] They cannot have employed large numbers, for in 1911 there were only eleven gunsmiths in Belfast. The firm still exists but has moved to Arthur Square; it still deals in guns but no longer makes them.

There were a few other groups of specialist smiths in the nineteenth century, such as anchor smiths and coach smiths, but their numbers amounted to only a few dozen in the whole of Ireland. The only comparatively large class of specialist smiths in the north of Ireland was the nailmakers. There were nailmakers in most towns and villages, and in the middle of the nineteenth century there were some 1,200 of them in what is now Northern Ireland, but the only places noted for nailmaking were Londonderry, Warrenpoint, and the village of Newtownbreda near Belfast. Like the blacksmiths, the nailmakers were seriously affected by the potato famine and its aftermath, and their numbers declined rapidly until in 1911 only fifty were still at work in the six counties which form Northern Ireland; these all went out of business in the next few years. Like their more numerous counterparts of the English Midlands, they could not withstand foreign competition and the introduction of machine-made nails. Machine competition arose in Belfast from 1874 when Wm Gregg, Sons & Phenix established a nail factory at Queen's Bridge; they used American self-feeding machines and were soon producing up to 2,000 tons of nails annually.[5] Nailmaking continued until the firm closed down in the early 1930s.

Wm Gregg, Sons & Phenix, Union Foundry, Belfast, 1882

The smiths had little chance of specialising; in no branch of production was local demand sufficient to permit division of labour of the kind long practised in the English Midlands, where particular towns specialised in making locks, stirrups, or nails of different types, or where the making of small-arms became the work of a large number of specialist crafts. They were either self-employed craftsmen dealing directly with their customers, or employees of large or small capitalists. There is no evidence that the 'putting out' system ever existed to any great extent. The local ironmongers did not attempt to organise production; instead they became the agents of British and overseas manufacturers supplying the Irish market in competition with the local producers of hardware.

There were too few cutlers, gunsmiths, or other specialist smiths in the north of Ireland to influence the development of the engineer-

Page 17   (left) Cast-iron lamp standard by Musgraves—with modern lantern; (right) Twin-cylinder vertical compound steam mill engine built by Victor Coates about 1890—adapted for rope driving

Page 18   (left) Stator for 3,000 hp electric motor for driving air compressor by Harland & Wolff Ltd; (right) 120 MW turbine-generator by AEI being installed at Ballylumford B power station

ing industry. The nailmakers were more numerous, but they were men who required little capital and they had no great skill; they were not the sort of people who could have been expected to embark on making steam engines or machinery. In 1857 it was said that nailmakers could become passable riveters in about a month at the Clyde shipbuilding yards,[6] but no evidence has come to light that many of them found work at this craft in the north of Ireland. They may, of course, have found semi-skilled or unskilled work in the engineering industry as it expanded. The blacksmiths were the only group of smiths important in the development of the industry in the north of Ireland, but their contribution was in building up the skilled labour force rather than in the establishment of new enterprises.

Millwrights

Corn mills were introduced into Ireland as early as the third century and became common in the north after the seventeenth century. In the second quarter of the eighteenth century, mills were developed for scutching, bleaching, and beetling linen, and there were mills for many other purposes such as the sawing of timber, extracting oil from seeds, or finishing woollen cloth. The machinery of these mills was constructed chiefly of wood, whether they were driven by water, wind, or horses. The millwrights who built and maintained them were itinerant craftsmen of considerable skill, for they had to be able to work in wood, stone, and iron, and understand how to provide an adequate water supply where this was the source of power. They have left few records of their activities in the north of Ireland during the seventeenth and eighteenth centuries. This may have been because they were men of small capital without workshops of their own, who worked at their customers' mills with materials supplied by the mill owners. According to Sir John Clapham, in the middle of the eighteenth century a millwright required less capital than a plasterer.[7] When cast iron was introduced for mill

B

gearing and machinery, the self-employed millwrights were displaced by engineering firms with a foundry and machine shop, as
well as erection and maintenance squads. Like the blacksmiths, the
millwrights were welcome recruits to the skilled labour force of the
early engineering industry, but few of them established engineering
firms of their own.

The only other important group of itinerant metalworkers carrying on business on their own account was that of the tinkers, who
worked in sheet metal. Until recent times their services were in
demand for making stills for the illicit production of spirits, but it
was not until the development of heating and ventilating plant that
sheetmetal workers began to be employed in substantial numbers by
some of the engineering firms in the north of Ireland.

Clockmakers

The first clockmaker in the north of Ireland appears to have been
John Bird, who set up business in Belfast about 1667. The trade did
not develop much before the middle of the eighteenth century, and
up to 1800 most Irish clockmakers worked in Dublin. After 1800,
clockmaking declined in Dublin, perhaps as a result of the Act of
Union, after which Dublin was no longer a capital city and many of
the nobility and gentry migrated to England. The Dublin trades
which catered for the moneyed classes suffered as a consequence, for
Dublin clocks were mostly expensive types with mahogany cases
and brass dials. In the north of Ireland the number of clockmakers
increased after 1800, and this may have been due partly to the fact
that they mainly produced cheap long-case clocks, with common
deal cases and painted iron dials, which were within the means of
the relatively prosperous local population.[8] From the middle of the
nineteenth century, the Irish clockmaking trade, both north and
south, declined rapidly with the import of cheap clocks from
America and the Continent, and thereafter almost all who called
themselves clockmakers were clock merchants or repairers rather

than makers of clocks. Even at their best, the northern Irish clock-makers were seldom more than assemblers of imported clock parts, for by the end of the eighteenth century specialists in the Liverpool region were supplying clockmakers throughout the British Isles with hands, wheels, pinions, springs, dials, and even complete clock movements.

Men who could assemble or even repair clocks required a high degree of skill. The clockmakers were, in many respects, the fore-runners of the modern mechanical engineers, and some of them played an important part in the development of the engineering industry in the north of Ireland, in the late eighteenth and early nineteenth centuries. Thomas McCabe, a watchmaker in North Street, Belfast, was concerned in the introduction of power spinning of cotton in Belfast. In 1842 Hugh Kennedy, a clockmaker, estab-lished the Coleraine Foundry where he made threshing and scutch-ing machines, and water turbines. The most talented of the local clockmakers was Job Rider, who made a number of remarkable clocks, one of which was wound by changes in atmospheric pressure; in partnership with another clockmaker, William Boyd, he estab-lished the Belfast Foundry in Donegall Street in 1811.

The clockmakers were the only group of independent craftsmen in the north of Ireland to make a significant contribution to the setting up of engineering works. Many who had been trained in clockmaking or repairing no doubt obtained employment in engi-neering, along with the smiths and millwrights, where their skill and knowledge of precision mechanisms were essential for future pro-gress.

CHAPTER THREE

Metal Founding

THE techniques used by the smiths, millwrights, and clockmakers could not have produced all the machinery required for the mechanisation of industry. For making frames and bed-plates for machines, and especially for complicated parts such as gear wheels, cast metal was more suitable than wrought iron or wood; it was particularly convenient when large numbers of identical parts had to be made. Nevertheless, cast iron proved to be brittle, and non-ferrous metals were expensive, so wrought iron and wood continued to be used in machine construction until the last quarter of the nineteenth century, when cheap steel became available for parts subject to shock and stress.

Ironfounding

Ironfounding became possible only with the development of the blast furnace, for earlier furnaces had reduced the ore to its metallic state without melting. Until the eighteenth century, the making of iron castings had to be carried out at the blast furnace, as there was no satisfactory way of remelting pig iron. Blast furnaces were introduced into Ireland in the seventeenth century, and while most of them produced pig iron for conversion into malleable wrought-iron bars, some ironfounding was carried on. In the south, cannon were made in the mid-seventeenth century; pots, pans, fire backs, and grave slabs were made in both north and south until the third quarter of the eighteenth century, by which time almost all the charcoal blast furnaces had gone out of production. The few blast furnaces in Ireland using coke in the first half of the nineteenth century were not successful and they did not establish any extensive ironfounding business.

The ironfounder became independent of the blast furnace in the first half of the eighteenth century, when small reverberatory or air furnaces began to be used to melt pig iron or scrap metal for recasting. It was some time before the new process was generally accepted, and not until 1760 that an ironfoundry was established in the north of Ireland. In that year Stewart Hadskis started an ironfoundry off Hill Street in Belfast, where he made pots and pans as well as boilers for the local bleachers. The business was carried on by the Hadskis family until 1798 when it was offered for sale, perhaps because of the political disturbances of the period, closing down shortly afterwards.[1]

A second foundry in Belfast was opened in 1783 by Benjamin Edwards, near his glassworks in Ballymacarrett. Edwards was a Bristol man, and before coming to Belfast had been superintendent of a glassworks at Drumrea, near Dungannon. The foundry was on a site at the junction of Newtownards Road and Foundry Street, which has been cleared in making the approaches for the new Lagan bridge. It produced bottle moulds and machinery for grinding materials for glassmaking, and later pots, pans, griddles, saucepans, kettles, yarn boilers, and equipment for papermills. In 1816 it was for sale along with another foundry which the Edwards family had set up at Newry in 1801, but seems to have found no purchaser prepared to carry on the ironfounding business, and to have closed down.[2]

The size of foundries increased when the steam engine came into use towards the end of the eighteenth century to power the blast for the cupola furnace which had replaced the air furnace for remelting pig iron. The cupola gave the foundryman stricter control over the composition of the metal, and it enabled larger castings to be made. The first large works was established in Belfast in 1799, if not a year earlier. In June 1799, McClenaghan, Stainton & Co informed the owners of bleach works and mills that their new foundry on the Short Strand at Ballymacarrett was fully prepared for making castings, and had been in operation for some time. In 1801 it was necessary to change the name to the 'Lagan Foundry' to avoid confusion with Edwards's premises, for orders for castings addressed to the new foundry were being delivered in error to Edwards's 'New Foundry' not far away. The address also changed after the building of the Albert Bridge when the Short Strand up-river from the bridge became part of the Ravenhill Road. When Edward Stainton died in 1802 the surviving partner, Victor Coates, carried on the business in his own name, and the firm subsequently became one of the best known in Belfast until it closed in 1905.[3]

In 1800 there were thus only two ironfoundries in Belfast, and it was not until 1811 that the Belfast Foundry was established in Donegall Street, and another was set up in Union Street by William Booth from Manchester.[4] There was no increase until the 1830s, when the numbers doubled; there followed a gradual increase to a maximum of twenty in 1870, and thereafter the numbers remained fairly constant until 1914. Throughout the nineteenth century Dublin was a more important ironfounding centre than Belfast, and in the first half of the century had twice as many foundries as Belfast.

Outside Belfast, the first ironfoundry in the north of Ireland appears to have been at Newry, opened at least as early as 1785;[5] it seems to have closed before another foundry was set up in the town in 1801 by the Edwards family, who were already engaged in iron-founding at Belfast. No further foundries were established in the area until the 1820s and then two were opened in Londonderry. Belfast, Newry, and Londonderry were the principal ports in the north of Ireland and the ironfounders there would have had ready access to supplies of raw materials and fuel by sea, as well as the advantage of selling their products from established commercial centres. The foundry which was set up at Doagh in county Antrim in 1824 by John Rowan & Sons was transferred to Belfast about 1846, having experienced transport difficulties. The firm of S. Gardiner & Co carried on ironfounding at Dobbin Street, Armagh, from 1840, if not earlier, until after 1880, and two other foundries were established at provincial towns in the north of Ireland in the

1840s. These were Kennedy's Coleraine Foundry opened in 1842, and the Strabane Foundry set up in 1843 by James Cooke & Co, which soon passed into the hands of the Stevenson family, and from the 1890s was owned by John A. Taylor & Son.

Between 1850 and 1880 the numbers of provincial ironfoundries doubled, and then increased gradually to a total of eighteen in 1914, by which time almost every substantial provincial town had at least one foundry. All were at railway centres, and although the railways provided a market for brake blocks and other castings, the deciding factor seems to have been transport facilities for raw materials and finished goods. The railways also helped to promote the growth of industry in the towns of eastern Ulster, and this helped to provide a market for castings. A few firms not situated on the railways called themselves 'foundries', but were in fact either spademills or smith-works.[6]

In the first half of the nineteenth century the Irish ironfounders were producing more iron goods for the local market than parts for machinery, and as yet competition from Britain was not severe. The trade naturally became concentrated in the old-established commercial centres, which were in the south rather than in the north. In the second half of the century increasing competition from British ironfounders, helped by improved transport facilities, curtailed the market for the southern firms, while the expanding engineering industry in Belfast and the north required more and more castings, and by the beginning of the twentieth century the great majority of Irish foundry workers, though not of foundries, were in the north.

Although pots and pans were made at the charcoal blast furnaces in the north of Ireland and later by the early Belfast ironfounders, the area did not become a centre for light ironfounding. Even before the beginning of the nineteenth century the British could undersell the Irish in their own market; it was said that the Irish founders made their pots heavier and therefore more costly.[7] Light iron-founding became a specialist technique and the Irish ironfounders with their limited local market were not able to specialise and so compete on anything like equal terms with those in Britain. Well before the middle of the nineteenth century, Falkirk ironfounders became the chief suppliers of light castings in the north of Ireland, especially of the three-legged pots now regarded as characteristically Irish. The local firms also found it difficult to compete with the specialists in architectural ironwork, whose profusely illustrated catalogues showed they could supply anything from a birdbath to a bandstand.

As far as general ironfounding was concerned, the firms in the north of Ireland were largely restricted to the local market for lamp-posts, manhole covers, railings, and similar castings requiring no great precision. They were well placed, however, to make heavy castings which were awkward and expensive to transport, such as the columns used in building local mills, theatres, and churches. They also had advantages over competitors from Britain for jobbing work, that is making castings to customers' instructions, often at short notice.

In Belfast, general ironfounders were never in the majority. In the 1830s only two of the eight ironfounders did not also engage in making steam engines or machinery, and in 1910 only two of the eighteen firms with foundries did not claim to make engines or machinery, though in some cases this was perhaps an intention rather than an established fact. In the 1960s only three of the dozen Belfast foundries could fairly be called general ironfounders. Iron-founding in Belfast became a subsidiary to the manufacture of land and marine engines or machinery, and all the large foundries were owned by engineering firms. Cast iron formed such a large consti-tuent of all nineteenth-century machines that a foundry was an essential part even of a relatively small works.

The provincial firms engaged in a wide range of work. James Stevenson of Strabane, for instance, in 1865 made machinery for flax and corn mills, threshing machines, water wheels, pumps, pil-lars, railings, and 'almost every other description of foundry work'.[8]

STRABANE FOUNDRY.

HAVING recently erected some additional Workshops, and otherwise improved the Foundry premises, I am now enabled, with increased facility, to execute any orders with which I may be entrusted.

FLAX SCUTCHING AND CORN MILL MACHINERY,

On the most approved principles;

FLAX ROLLERS,

Of various kinds, with latest improvements;

WATER WHEELS, THRASHING MACHINES,

Auction and Force Pumps; Retorts, &c. for Gas Works,

PILLARS,

PLAIN AND ORNAMENTAL RAILING,

WATER AND STOVE PIPES, EAVE GUTTERS,

SPADE-MAKERS' TOOLS,

FARM BOILERS, PIG TROUGHS,

Plough Mounting, Sash and Scale Weights,

Window Sashes, for Churches, Cottages, &c.,

FARM YARD BELLS, MILL BRASSES, &c.,

With almost every other description of FOUNDRY WORK, executed with despatch, and on Moderate Terms.

Turning, Boring, Mill-Wright & Smith Work of all kinds, EXECUTED IN THE BEST MANNER.

Mill Machinery erected and repaired by experienced Workmen.

Strabane, June, 1865.

JAMES STEVENSON.

Most provincial foundries seemed to be prepared to make any fairly simple article in cast iron if the work promised to be profitable. In the 1840s Gardiners of Armagh were making cast-iron coffins, which had been made popular by the great early English ironfounders Abraham Darby and John Wilkinson.[9] With increasing competition, the provincial firms were restricted to castings and relatively simple machinery for the local market, but they could provide a jobbing and millwright service in their immediate locality more quickly than firms from Britain or even Belfast. Most of them made and erected corn mills, threshing and churning machines, flax scutch mills, and equipment for linen bleaching. Many of them also erected water wheels, but only a few made water turbines or steam engines. Their restricted market and their consequent inability to specialise in any one line of manufacture, made the future of most of them insecure even before 1914.

Whilst the first world war brought additional work to the iron-founders, it was followed in Ireland by political disturbances and by the division of the country into two separate states, and those firms in the north which had done business in the south found themselves cut off from their southern customers. Unfortunately for the iron-founders, the depressions of the 1920s and 1930s coincided with the adoption of new techniques which lessened the demand for cast iron. Concrete began to be used more extensively for structural work and even began to replace cast iron for lamp-posts. Welded structures were used increasingly in place of castings. In the 1920s and 1930s, a number of firms in Belfast which had once been well known as general ironfounders, such as Victor C. Taylor and the Millfield Foundry, went out of business. Other foundries closed when the engineering works to which they were attached ceased production. Between the end of the first world war and the commencement of the second, the number of foundries in Belfast had been reduced from twenty to fourteen. In the same period the foundries closed in Newry and Strabane. The second world war brought another surge of business, and it was followed by a period in which the foundries in the north of Ireland even found it possible to obtain orders for castings in Britain, but the replacement of cast iron by other materials continued. Some of the Belfast engineering works closed their foundries, some of the provincial firms went out of business, and others continued to call themselves 'foundries' although ironfounding had been reduced to a small fraction of the firm's production. By the 1960s, the only provincial towns with ironfoundries were Coleraine, Larne, Lisburn, Londonderry, and Portadown.

Only a few of the engineering firms established in the north of Ireland since the war have set up foundries, but from the middle of the 1950s existing engineering firms have begun to re-equip their foundries, or in some cases to establish new ones, with a view especially to the production of light castings or malleable forms of cast iron. It would seem that the trend away from the use of cast iron in engineering has been arrested for the present at least, and that most of the dozen foundries in Belfast and the half-dozen in the provincial towns will be able to continue in business, assuming of course that their production is efficient.

Although ironfounding was an important factor in the growth of the engineering industry in the north of Ireland, its contribution was in the production of plant and machinery, rather than through general ironfounding. Since both pig iron and fuel had to be imported the trade operated under disadvantages, and the region was not an ideal location for iron foundries. This point is demonstrated by the fact that both of the large Belfast firms of shipbuilders and marine engineers, Harland & Wolff and Workman Clark, found it advantageous to establish foundries on the Clyde. Though general ironfounders did not flourish in the north of Ireland they had one advantage over most other firms in the engineering industry; they were privileged to erect monuments to themselves at public expense through inscribing their names prominently on their products. A study of lamp-posts, manhole covers, and other easily accessible castings, now provides almost the only record of the activities of

foundries which have been closed for many years and whose written
records have perished.

Brassfounding

Bronzefounding, using an alloy of copper and tin, was developed
in prehistoric times, and was carried on through the middle ages by
the bellfounders. There were bellfounders in Carrickfergus and Belfast in the seventeenth and eighteenth centuries, after which Irish
bellfounding became concentrated in Dublin. Brassfounding, using
an alloy of copper and zinc, was not established in the British Isles
until the seventeenth century, and there were few brassfounders in
the north of Ireland until the end of the next century. Andrew Law
commenced business in Belfast in 1777 as a plumber and brassfounder; he was the first of many who combined the two crafts and
later added gasfitting to their activities. After 1800, the trade increased steadily, through the demand for brasswork for steam engines, machinery, and ships, the introduction of gas lighting and
public water supply, as well as the nineteenth-century fashion for
brass ornaments. The market for local makers of small brass castings
was greatly reduced by the 1880s by the extension of the factory
system in Britain, and by the substitution of stamping and pressing
for casting. The large firms which made steam engines or textile
machinery, and the shipbuilders, undertook brassfounding to provide the brass parts which they required, many of which had originally been supplied by the specialist brassfounders.

In the provincial towns there were a few independent brassfounders during the nineteenth century, but by the beginning of the
present century brassfounding outside Belfast was carried on only at
the ironfoundries. In Belfast some seventy-five brassfoundries were
set up between 1820 and 1870, and over thirty of them survived less
than two years, and many of the others did not fare much better. By
1914 there were still a dozen independent brassfoundries, but in the
1960s there were only three, although most of the ironfounders also

carried on brassfounding. Less equipment and material, and therefore less capital were required for brassfounding than for ironfounding, and in each workshop only a few men were employed. Brassfounding in the nineteenth century was a 'backyard' trade and many
of the Belfast firms moved their equipment frequently from one
residential part of the town to another. It was comparatively easy to
set up in business, but it certainly does not appear to have been a
stable or prosperous trade, once competition from Britain began to
be felt. In recent times it has been less subject to fluctuations,
though greatly reduced in size, and, like ironfounding, has become a
subsidiary of engineering rather than a separate industry.

Other Metals

Steelfounding developed in the last quarter of the nineteenth
century, but has not been established successfully in the north of
Ireland. It is a more difficult and expensive operation than ironfounding, and there was no tradition of steelmaking in the area to
encourage its development. The demand for steel castings is probably too small and the variety too great at present to make steelfounding in the province profitable. The steel foundry which was set
up at the former railway workshops at Dundalk in 1958, and which
supplied steel castings to some firms in Belfast and the north, closed
down in 1966.

Aluminium castings were being produced in Belfast in 1909 but it
was not until after the second world war that the technique was
widely adopted, generally by firms which already had iron or brass
foundries. In only one or two cases did firms regularly produce
aluminium castings for general sale. It is not strictly correct to
classify plastic mouldings with metal castings, but they are produced
by some engineering firm by similar techniques, to replace metal or
wooden components. Again they are a means to an end in the north
of Ireland, rather than an end in themselves.

It would be fair to say that while the founders in the north of

Ireland did supply a local demand for castings early in the nine-teenth century, from the second half of the century they have come more and more to supply components for engineering firms, and only a small number of founders are producing castings for sale as such.

CHAPTER FOUR

Power Plant

ALL power-using industries need prime movers to drive their machinery, so there was a widespread demand for power plant once the industrial revolution gathered momentum. Until the latter part of the nineteenth century, power plant, whether moved by water, wind, or steam, was heavy and difficult to transport and there were advantages in making it as near as possible to where it was to be used. This is a reason why the production of power plant was the first branch of the modern engineering industry to develop in the north of Ireland.

Water Power

Water wheels were the chief source of power for industry well into the nineteenth century, but by then their construction had passed from the itinerant millwrights to the newly established engineering firms. In Belfast, little water power was available, as the city is built on a flat site only a few feet above sea level; the industries using water power were either on the outskirts of the city or in the countryside, and thus the making and repair of water wheels was mainly in the hands of the provincial firms. The Belfast firms which undertook millwright work also made water wheels, but this was for them a sideline rather than a major activity. Water power had to be used where the contours of the land dictated, in places not necessarily otherwise suited for industrial purposes. The user of water power was at the mercy of floods and frost in winter and droughts in summer, which interfered with his power supply, and there was considerable difficulty in governing the speed of water wheels to ensure the steady output of power necessary for many purposes, such as power-loom weaving. In spite of these disadvantages water wheels continued to provide a suitable source of power for small mills, especially those which were not required to run continuously, for the water supply and water wheel were not expensive to maintain once they had been installed. Few new water wheels were erected in the twentieth century, but those in existence at the beginning of the century went out of use only gradually with the closing of corn or scutch mills, or the replacement of water power by electricity or internal combustion engines.

By the beginning of the twentieth century, however, the turbine had replaced the water wheel for driving machinery in the larger mills where water power was still used. The development of the water turbine after 1827, when Fourneyron produced his first successful machine, made possible the more efficient use of water power. Higher falls could be harnessed, and the power output could be governed more effectively. In the second half of the nineteenth century a number of individuals and firms in the north of Ireland helped in the improvement of the water turbine. James Thomson, the second Professor of Engineering at Queen's College, Belfast, developed his inward flow 'Vortex' turbine, with coupled pivoted guide vanes which governed partial loads with little loss of efficiency. These were widely used in the north of Ireland after their introduction in the early 1850s, and were made by Victor Coates & Co at the Lagan Foundry as well as by makers in Britain. Turbines designed by William Cullen of Armagh were made by MacAdam Brothers at the Soho Foundry in Belfast, and some turbines were made by S. Gardiner & Co of Armagh. H. Kennedy & Son of Coleraine introduced their 'Empress' turbines about 1880, and these continued to be made until 1953; in Belfast, Francis-type turbines were made by Robert Craig & Sons from 1921 until the early 1960s. A few turbines may have been made at Derrymore Foundry in Bessbrook, but the other firms in the north of Ireland which advertised themselves as suppliers of turbines probably installed machines made elsewhere. The majority of the locally made turbines were

Page 35   (above) *Cord laying machine;* (below) *Hemp softener, by James Reynolds & Co Ltd*

Page 36   (above) *Flax or hemp hackling machine fitted to automatic spreader;* (below) *Ring spinning frame for man-made fibres and wool, by James Mackie & Sons Ltd*

installed in linen and flax mills, bleach works, or corn mills in the north of Ireland, but the local firms did not have the market all to themselves, for many turbines used in the area were made in Britain, Europe, or America.[1]

Some nineteenth-century commentators accused the Irish of letting their water power run to waste, but the power of some rivers at least in the north of Ireland was well exploited. Pioneering work was done in the use of water power to generate electricity for traction, on the tramways from Portrush to the Giant's Causeway and from Bessbrook to Newry, but the region did not make much further progress in the development of hydro-electricity in the twentieth century, for there are no sites in the north of Ireland suitable for large-scale generating stations comparable with those on the Continent, in America, and in the north of Scotland.

Wind

In the north of Ireland windmills were much less numerous than watermills, and there were few in any Ulster county except Down.[2] Very little information exists about the men who built them, probably itinerant millwrights until well into the nineteenth century, when the ironfounders began to supply part at least of the machinery. The gearing was usually an interesting mixture of wheels wholly of cast iron, wooden wheels with cast-iron teeth, and cast-iron wheels with teeth of wood. Most of the windmills had gone out of use before 1900, with the exception of small units used to pump water on farms.

Horse Power

Before the development of steam power, men who could not make use of water or wind had to harness their domestic animals if they did not wish to depend on their own muscles to operate machinery. Some of the early Belfast cotton mills were worked by horses, but

c

the use of horse power for factories soon proved inadequate. For many purposes connected with agriculture, however, where little power was needed and that only for short periods, horse power was the cheapest available until the invention of the internal combustion engine. Threshing and churning machines made by the provincial

Horse-operated churn by H. Kennedy & Son Ltd, Coleraine

ironfounders were horse powered, and at some farms the remains of the track are still to be seen where the horse walked round and round, harnessed to the arm which operated the machinery.

Steam

The first reliable steam engine was the atmospheric beam engine, introduced by Thomas Newcomen in the second decade of the eighteenth century. The early steam engines were not suitable for driving rotating machinery, but were used for pumping water, chiefly from mines, and as there was very limited mining activity in the north of Ireland it was not until 1786 that the first steam pumping engine was erected in the area, at Drumglass colliery in county Tyrone.[3] One of the earliest methods for driving machinery by a reciprocating steam engine was to use a pumping engine to return water to the top of a water wheel. This avoided having to make any alteration in the existing power transmission and allowed the steam engine to be used only when there was insufficient water supply. The first steam engine erected in Belfast was at Springfield cotton mill, and was used from about 1790 for pumping water to drive a water wheel. Some pumping engines were made in Belfast; about 1846 MacAdam Brothers made several large engines which were used in Egypt to pump water from the Nile for irrigation.[4] This was not because the firm had any special expertise in the making of steam engines. They had made contacts with the Egyptians through the export of flax scutching machinery and no doubt this led to the order for the pumping engines. At that period any large engineering firm would have been prepared to undertake the construction of all types of machinery, including steam engines, if they could secure designs or machines to copy, for specialisation did not become general until the second half of the nineteenth century.

Watt's improved steam engine consumed only a quarter of the coal used by the Newcomen engine, and it was quickly adapted to drive rotating machinery. From the 1780s it provided motive power in textile mills, and in the north of Ireland it was in the cotton industry that the steam engine was first used for driving machinery directly. James Wallace set up a cotton mill in Lisburn in 1790 on a site where water power was not available, and he obtained a 15 hp Boulton & Watt engine to drive the mill. Thereafter, the introduction of steam power in the area was a gradual process; from 1800 to 1812 fifteen steam engines of 212 hp were erected within a 10 mile radius of Belfast. Impetus was given to the use of steam power in the cotton industry by the dependence on imported raw material, which encouraged the location of the mills in Belfast and on the coast of Antrim and Down, often on sites where water power could not be used. The cotton industry in the north of Ireland declined rapidly in the second quarter of the nineteenth century, but from the early 1830s power spinning was applied to linen. In 1838 there were in Belfast eighteen steam engines of 690 hp used for spinning linen, and only three engines of 92 hp for spinning cotton. There were also six steam engines in foundries, four in grain mills, four employed in textile finishing, and over a dozen engaged on a wide variety of processes from making paper and whiskey to grinding coffee. More than half the horse power available was concentrated in the linen industry, spinning yarn for the hand-loom weavers.[5]

In 1838, Belfast had a total of fifty steam engines, more than any other Irish town, and about a third of the total number in Ireland. More important, the number of new installations per year had been increasing more rapidly in Belfast from the early 1830s, and this helped to bring about the transfer of the main centre of steam-engine making in Ireland from Dublin to Belfast in the second quarter of the century. Not only were steam engines difficult and expensive to transport; to be efficient they had to be designed for the particular circumstances in which they were to work. This, no doubt, encouraged the Belfast ironfounders to embark on making them when the local demand began to increase, and gave them advantages over competitors from Britain.

Job Rider, a Belfast clockmaker, offered his services as works superintendent at Wallace's cotton mill in Lisburn when the machinery was being erected.[6] It is not clear whether his offer was accepted because he was already an expert on steam power, or whether his action was prompted by a desire to find out more about a Boulton & Watt engine at close quarters. By 1805 he had patented a number of improvements in steam engines. To solve the problem of making accurate cylinders, which was one of the chief difficulties facing the early steam-engine makers, he proposed lining the cylinders with a soft metal such as pewter, and finishing the inside surface by 'draw boring'; he also had in mind using hollow piston rods as eduction pipes, and regulating the speed of the engine by means of a pendulum. In 1820 he patented a novel type of rotary steam engine which he claimed would operate without a flywheel, but there is no record of its successful production.[7] Job Rider was probably the moving spirit behind the manufacture of steam engines at the Belfast Foundry in Donegall Street from its establishment in 1811. The firm continued to make steam engines until the 1850s.

A steam engine of their own manufacture was being erected by Victor Coates & Co at their Lagan Foundry in 1812, and in 1823 the firm had a boring machine for finishing the cylinders of steam engines; it was claimed that only one other similar machine existed in Ireland. This was an important acquisition, for it was John Wilkinson's invention of a new type of boring machine that had made possible the production of cylinders accurate enough for Watt's improved engine. In 1848 it was said that no part of England could produce better steam engines than those made at the Lagan Foundry.[8] In the 1850s, MacAdam Brothers and John Rowan & Sons had joined Victor Coates as steam-engine makers, and in the 1880s Combe, Barbour & Combe of the Falls Foundry added steam-engine making to their existing activities. By 1900 MacAdam and Rowan had gone out of business, and in 1905 Victor Coates closed down, leaving the Falls Foundry as the only maker of large steam engines in the north of Ireland, apart from the marine engineering firms. After the making of steam engines at the Falls Foundry came to an end early in the 1920s, no large steam engines were made outside the marine engine works until the turbine generator works was set up at Larne in 1956. Towards the end of the nineteenth century perhaps a dozen firms were making small steam engines, mostly in Belfast but also in Newry and Strabane. Although the market for large engines to drive complete mills was already declining, a new market had grown up for small engines, especially high-speed engines to drive ventilating fans or electric generators. Small steam engines continued to be made in Belfast until the late 1930s, by which time electric motors or internal combustion engines had almost entirely replaced them.

The great majority of steam engines made in the north of Ireland were for local customers, and it is probable that the few which were exported attracted publicity because they were exceptions to the general rule. For instance, in 1899 the Falls Foundry produced two quadruple-expansion engines for cotton mills in India, and in the early years of the present century they made an engine for Huddersfield Corporation. Only a few years before they closed, Victor Coates & Co completed a 3,000 hp triple-expansion engine to generate electricity for the Newcastle-upon-Tyne tramways.[9]

For most of the nineteenth century, where water power was available, steam continued to be used mainly to supplement water wheels or turbines. As additional equipment was introduced to meet the rising demand for power, assorted power plants came into existence, using water wheels, turbines, and differing types of steam engines, and many continued in use well into the present century. In the last quarter of the nineteenth century the demand for steam engines began to decrease with the introduction of electric motors and internal combustion engines, but the reasons for this were not always obvious to those engaged in the trade. In 1905, the Belfast employers complained that the making of steam engines had declined in the city over the past thirty years, and that this had led to the closure of the two largest firms, presumably Rowan and Coates, which thirty years earlier had between them executed practically all the work on steam engines in Ireland. The employers felt that the high wage rates in Belfast made their prices uncompetitive, but it is more likely that the local firms were at a disadvantage, technically as well as commercially, in competing with larger and more specialised engine makers, especially in a declining market.

No Belfast firm carried on the tradition of innovation established by Job Rider in the first quarter of the nineteenth century. No 'Belfast engine' was developed, but attention was devoted to a number of the details of steam engine construction and some of the products which resulted had a continuing demand even after the making of steam engines in Belfast had come to an end. In 1856 James Combe of the Falls Foundry developed the method of transmitting power by means of ropes running in V-shaped grooves in pulleys or in the rim of the engine flywheel.[10] This method of power transmission was extensively used in textile mills until the introduction of electric motors, and later led to the development of modern V-belt drives. Improved piston rings were made by a number of Belfast firms, but those which have stood the test of time and are still being made were invented by William Rowan and improved by John Hind;[11] they are manufactured by Rowan's successors, John Hind & Sons Ltd.

The making of steam engines was an important stage in the development of the engineering industry in the north of Ireland. It made the firms and workers in the area familiar with the metal-working techniques necessary for the production of machinery, and, along with ironfounding, provided capacity for the exploitation of opportunities to make other types of equipment when the demand for steam engines declined. Marine engineering followed a different pattern and will be dealt with separately.

Internal Combustion Engines

One of the causes of the decline in the demand for steam engines was the development of the gas engine. These engines were economical when intermittent running was required, and particularly suitable for small works. They were not made in the north of Ireland, but a number of local firms were active in selling and installing them. Petrol engines were made by Chambers Motors Ltd of Belfast for their early motor cars, but later models were fitted with engines imported from Britain. Motor-car engines were not subsequently made in the area, and it was not until the 1960s that components such as carburettors and exhaust systems began to be made. In 1966 Rolls-Royce established a factory at Dundonald on the outskirts of Belfast to produce small steel components for aero engines. Small diesel engines for commercial vehicles have not been manufactured in the north of Ireland, but from the middle of the 1930s Harland & Wolff have built large numbers of medium-sized diesel engines for rail locomotives, pumping stations, electricity generating, and ships' auxiliary machinery.

Electricity

Public electricity supply and the use of electric motors to provide individual drives for machines finally displaced the steam engine as the source of power in factories. The flexibility and economy of this system were so great that by 1914 few firms would consider installing a steam engine for direct driving. It was still a moot point whether it was better to generate a private supply of electricity or to depend on the public supply, where one was available, but with the extension of the electricity distribution system from the 1930s private electrical generating plants gradually went out of use.

A number of people in the north of Ireland experimented with electrical equipment in the last quarter of the nineteenth century and by 1883 J. H. Greenhill had begun the commercial production of dynamos in Belfast, and subsequently manufactured electric motors. The firm of Hugh J. Scott & Co, which had been formed in 1855 to manufacture chemicals and later became shipowners, began in 1900 to make electric motors and dynamos at Ravenhill Avenue in Belfast, and the business expanded until by the 1960s a wide range of AC and DC motors and generators were being produced, as well as instructional sets for technical colleges. Early in the 1920s Harland & Wolff set up workshops for the production of electric motors, generators, and equipment for ships, and later undertook work for outside customers. One or two other firms made electric motors in Belfast in the 1920s, but by the 1960s only three firms were still making them, Hugh J. Scott, Harland & Wolff, and Jennings Electric (Belfast) Ltd. Few firms in the north of Ireland have made fractional horse-power motors, the principal maker being BVC at Castlereagh in Belfast; for a time in the 1960s they were also made by AEI at Larne. The electric motors made in the north of Ireland have been used mainly to drive pumps, fans, hoists, and looms, and in ships especially for steering gear, but they have been applied to a very wide range of purposes, particularly in wartime. A large proportion have been exported. The firms making electric motors have also provided a repair service for local users of motors and small generators.

The large generators required for public electricity supply and the steam turbines to drive them were not made in the north of Ireland until the 1950s when the British Thomson Houston Company, later AEI Turbine-Generators Ltd, established works at Larne in county Antrim. A factory for the manufacture of turbine blades was opened in 1955 and the main turbine factory in 1956. The turbines produced have been mainly medium-size, or large low-speed, low-pressure units of the type used in nuclear power stations. The associated generators have also been made at Larne, but the generator rotors have usually been supplied from the other works belonging to the company. While most of the equipment produced has been exported from the province, by the early 1970s the greater part of the generating capacity of the Electricity Board for Northern Ireland will be powered by turbines built at Larne. Five 60 MW turbine generators have been installed at Coolkeeragh Power Station, and three 120 MW sets are being installed at Ballylumford B Power Station, to be followed by three 200 MW units.

CHAPTER FIVE

Textile Machinery

THE engineering firms in the north of Ireland apparently had little difficulty in making steam engines when a local market for them developed at the beginning of the nineteenth century. They encountered many problems, however, in producing machinery for the textile industry.

Cotton Spinning

The cotton industry was established in the south of Ireland as early as 1750, and had made progress even before the Irish Government started to encourage it by bounties and protective duties in 1782. In the late 1770s cotton spinning was introduced to provide work for the poorhouse children in Belfast, and soon afterwards spinning mills were built in and near the city. By 1800 there were eleven cotton mills in Belfast and neighbourhood, and by 1811 the number within a 10 mile radius had risen to thirty-three. In the second quarter of the century, cotton spinning declined after the removal of the protecting duties, for the industry had depended almost entirely on the Irish market.[1] It did not die out completely in the north of Ireland, but after 1850 there were never more than half a dozen cotton mills in the area.

Though the industry declined, its influence was important. It encouraged the immigration of British entrepreneurs who brought capitalist organisation and the use of power-driven machinery to the local spinning industry; these contributed to the development of the linen industry after the decline of cotton. The manufacture of cotton-spinning machinery was not established in the north of Ireland, however, despite machinery's introduction at the inception of the local cotton industry.

46

In the early days of the textile industry each mill owner usually had his machinery made on the premises. It was some time before a few firms abandoned yarn production and specialised in the making of machines, and some engineering firms mastered the difficulties encountered in producing textile machinery. When Henry and Robert Joy, Thomas McCabe, and John McCracken were investigating the possibility of spinning cotton in Belfast, one of the partners went to England and acquired an intimate knowledge of the trade at considerable expense, and also at much personal risk on account of the jealousy of the English manufacturers.[2] Industrial espionage is no new thing! The assistance was secured of Nicholas Grimshaw, a cotton printer from Lancashire, and under his guidance a spinning machine was made, and an experienced spinner brought over from Scotland to instruct the poorhouse children in its operation. Subsequently, carding machines and improved spinning machines were made and shown freely to anyone who was interested. Some local inventors may have turned their attention to cotton machinery, for Nathaniel Wilson of Belfast advanced £3,000 to finance a man who had invented a 'water-mill for spinning warp cotton of a similar quality to that spun by Mr. Arkwright'. They had a small mill at work in 1782 and a larger one in 1783.[3]

A few small works were established near Belfast early in the nineteenth century to provide parts for cotton-spinning machines, especially spindles, but there were no makers of cotton machinery in the region until the industry had passed the peak of its prosperity. In 1820 Victor Coates & Co announced that they had recently erected an improved furnace at their Lagan Foundry for the sole purpose of casting parts for cotton and other mill machinery which would be equal if not superior to anything which could be imported.[4] The new furnace was no doubt useful for other purposes, but it was too late to serve the demand caused by the expansion of the local cotton industry, and Coates appear to have abandoned making cotton machinery soon afterwards.

Cotton Weaving

After the introduction of cotton spinning, most of the handloom weavers in Belfast and its vicinity changed over from linen to cotton, for the earnings of cotton weavers were considerably higher and cotton was easier to weave. When cotton spinning declined in the second quarter of the nineteenth century, cotton weaving did not decline to anything like the same extent. The low wages for which the Ulster weavers were willing to work encouraged Glasgow manufacturers to give out yarn to be woven, and until the cotton famine of the 1860s the Belfast region became the weaving workshop of Glasgow. The making of handlooms was the work of various groups of self-employed craftsmen, joiners, reed-makers, heddle-makers, and shuttle-makers, and never showed any tendency to develop into a large-scale industry.

Cotton power looms were in use in Belfast by 1815, but the availability of cheap handloom labour hindered their widespread introduction, and in the late 1830s there was still only one cotton power-loom factory in Belfast and none elsewhere in the north of Ireland. Cotton weaving by power was not firmly established in Belfast until the 1850s; it was severely affected by the cotton famine caused by the American civil war, and after the 1860s cotton weaving remained a relatively small section of the textile industry in the north of Ireland. There was nothing to encourage local engineering firms to attempt making cotton power looms in competition with the English specialists.[5]

Linen

The concentration of the Irish linen industry in the north-east of the country had begun long before it was affected by the industrial revolution. The chief reason appears to have been the greater security of tenure enjoyed by the Ulster tenant farmers. This made possible the accumulation of capital which enabled farmer-manu-facturers to give out yarn to be woven or to employ weavers directly, and led to the rise of the bleachers to prominence in the organisation of linen production, so that some of them were in a position to make use of power-driven machinery when it became available.[6]

Flax Scutching

The raw material for the cotton industry had been imported; for a long time, part at least of the flax supply for the linen industry was grown locally, and therefore tools and machinery were needed to extract the fibre from the plants. Flax is a bast fibre, from the stem of the flax plant, and has to be freed from the core by retting, or steeping in water. When the retted plants are dried, the stems can easily be broken and the unwanted parts beaten off by hand or machinery in the process called 'scutching'.

Hand scutching continued so long as linen yarn was spun in the home, and this was done only to a small extent after the second quarter of the nineteenth century. Scutch mills were in use as early as 1717 and were more generally adopted about 1750; the number of scutch mills at work depended on the acreage of the flax crop rather than on the prosperity or otherwise of the linen industry, and in spite of efforts to encourage the wider growth of flax the crop gradually decreased. The number of scutch mills in Ulster reached its maximum of over 1,400 in 1868, as a result of the expansion of the linen industry following the shortage of cotton, but had declined to about 600 by 1914. The linen industry came to depend more and more on imported flax, chiefly from Belgium and Russia, and the expansion of flax growing during both world wars was a temporary measure made necessary by the interruption of imports; the decline in acreage resumed as soon as imported flax again became available. The number of scutch mills in Northern Ireland had fallen to less than 300 in 1939, and while new mills were built and old ones reopened during the war, the fall in numbers continued with the return of peacetime conditions, and by the end of the 1950s flax growing and scutching had practically ceased in the north of Ireland. Flax was reckoned to be exhausting to the soil, but the chief disadvantage for the cultivator was that it had to be pulled by hand, for otherwise a substantial part of the fibre would have been lost. Mechanical flax pullers were widely used in Belgium and France, but they did not prove very successful under the rather different conditions in which flax was grown in the north of Ireland. Retting on the farm was also a difficult and unpleasant process, and good results could be obtained only if it was managed properly, while tank retting was expensive. Attempts were being made to revive flax growing in 1968, when some 100 acres were sown in Antrim and Down, but it remains to be seen whether this will prove successful when so many similar projects in the past have failed.

A great deal of effort and money was spent by the Irish Linen Board in trying to improve flax-scutching machinery, especially in the first quarter of the nineteenth century, but at the end of the century it was generally admitted that all attempts to popularise better scutching machinery had failed, and the old vertical scutch mill, with some modifications, remained in use until flax-scutching ceased. Most improved scutching machines demanded flax of uniform quality and this was seldom available in the north of Ireland. There were attractions in scutching flax without the usual retting, and many attempted to perfect this process. Green scutching was undertaken extensively during the second world war, when fibre output had to be increased rapidly, but the cost was high and the fibre produced of low quality, and the process was largely abandoned soon afterwards.

Scutching machinery was made by some of the Belfast engineering firms, but the making of scutch-mill machinery was undertaken mainly by the provincial firms, especially Kennedy of Coleraine and Taylor of Strabane. The manufacture was well suited to small unspecialised works, as a high degree of accuracy was not required. The flax-breaking machine consisted of a series of fluted iron rollers

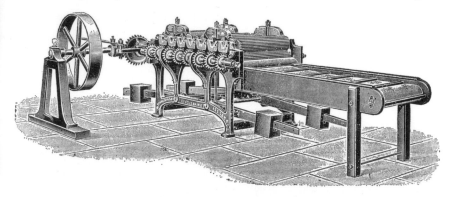

Flax-breaking machine by H. Kennedy & Son Ltd, Coleraine

through which the flax was passed. The scutching machine was even simpler: the broken stems were beaten off the flax fibre as it was held over a board or stock by a number of wooden blades attached to a rotating shaft. The water wheel, transmission, and gearing probably accounted for as much of the capital cost of a scutch-mill as the actual breaking and scutching machinery. By the 1840s, scutching machinery had been exported to Egypt, Germany, and France, and by the middle of the century the north of Ireland had become the leading producer of scutch-mill equipment. The local firms lost most of their export markets in the second half of the nineteenth century with increasing competition, and with the reduction in the number of scutch-mills at home the making of their machinery declined, once the wartime demand had been met.

Flax Carding and Hackling

Long-staple flax fibre, called 'line', has to be hackled or combed after it is scutched, before being ready for spinning. Shorter flax fibres, such as those removed during hackling, are called 'tow'; these are spun into coarse yarn and prepared for spinning on carding machines similar to those used for cotton. In the north of Ireland, the attempts to spin flax by power before the 1820s were largely confined to yarns made from short tow fibres, as suitable machinery had not then been developed for spinning fine yarns from long-staple flax. Carding machines were in use in the area by the first decade of the nineteenth century for tow preparation, but there is no record of their being made in the north of Ireland until after 1850. Some were imported from Britain and some were obtained from Dublin, where cotton machinery had been made in the eighteenth century and where the machine makers would have been familiar with the construction of carding machines. When carding machines began to be made in the north of Ireland, they were produced only by the large textile machinery firms, like Mackies and the Falls Foundry.

Until the middle of the nineteenth century the hackling of long-fibre flax continued to be done by hand, for the evolution of an efficient hackling machine took a long time; even after the introduction of hackling machines, it was necessary to do the preliminary roughing by hand. The machines in use up to 1850 seem to have been imported, mainly from Leeds, but by 1853 James Combe & Co were making hackling machines at the Falls Foundry in Belfast, and soon afterwards their development was greatly advanced by two men who came to Belfast from Leeds. George Horner served his apprenticeship with Samuel Lawson & Sons in Leeds, and after six years with James Combe & Co in Belfast, he started business on his own account at the Clonard Foundry in 1859, specialising in making hackling machines for flax and hemp. He claimed to have made over 2,000 between 1859 and 1890 and to have sold them in the United Kingdom, on the Continent and in America. Horner was best known for his 'Duplex' machine, which hackled both ends of the flax, and took up much less room than a pair of single machines; he also made a 'Giant' machine capable of hackling hemp over 6 ft long.[7] The firm continued in business until 1905, when it was acquired by James Mackie & Sons Ltd.

Stephen Cotton came to Belfast in 1865 and established his

Page 53 (left) 17,000 ihp four crank triple expansion marine steam engines by Harland & Wolff—as fitted (with low-pressure turbine) to Olympic, Titanic and Britannic; (right) Set of twenty-four double-ended and five single-ended coal-fired boilers by Harland & Wolff as fitted to Olympic, Titanic and Britannic

Page 54   (above) 23,000 bhp ten-cylinder H&W–B&W diesel engine for MV Borgsten; (below)
30,000 shp double reduction geared steam turbines by Harland & Wolff for oil tanker Myrin

Brookfield Foundry, where at first he made spinning and drawing frames as well as hackling machines. The demand for hackling machines led him to concentrate on producing them, although he also made roller-fluting machines, power reels, and bundling presses. Cotton claimed that his machine was less severe on the flax than Horner's and far less noisy; although opinion in the linen trade was divided,[8] Cotton's machine was the type which continued to be made, for Horner's did not prove suitable for the addition of later automatic attachments. Stephen Cotton & Co Ltd continued making hackling machines until 1962, when the company went into voluntary liquidation. Since the production of textile machinery at the Falls Foundry came to an end in 1955, the only makers of hackling machines in Belfast after 1962 were James Mackie & Sons Ltd.

The making of hackling machines was a much more specialised business than the production of scutching machinery. In the north of Ireland it was confined entirely to Belfast and was carried on by only three firms at any one time. This specialisation helped to produce machines of advanced design, with many patented improvements. Some of these, and in particular the automatic screwing devices which eliminated the need for boys to screw and unscrew the flax holders, were the result of close co-operation between the technical staff of the linen firms and the machine makers. Though the development of hackling machines was slow up to 1850, progress was rapid in the next twenty years; while most of those in use in the north of Ireland had come from Leeds up to 1850, by the end of the 1860s Leeds spinners were beginning to buy them in Belfast. Soon afterwards hackling machines were being exported from Belfast to the principal flax-spinning countries on the Continent—France, Russia, Germany, Belgium, and Austria-Hungary.

Flax Preparing and Spinning

Unlike cotton, power-spun from its introduction into the area, flax had been spun by hand in the north of Ireland for centuries

D

before the industrial revolution. Hand spinning declined very rapidly after the introduction of power spinning for fine counts of yarn in the second quarter of the nineteenth century, but it continued on a small scale long after it had ceased to provide any adequate financial reward, probably because it was done by the farmers' wives in their spare time. There was an outlet for handspun yarn so long as handloom weaving continued to be a domestic industry, as it was in some parts of the north of Ireland up to the last decade of the nineteenth century. By the end of the century there appears to have been only one firm of spinning-wheel makers still in operation in Belfast, but they were carvers in bog oak and makers of 'antique' spinning-wheels and bric-à-brac, makers of spinning-wheels for use as ornaments rather than for work.

In hand spinning the fibres were drawn out between the index finger and thumb before being twisted. During the eighteenth century it was possible to solve the problem of how to do this by machinery for the short fibres of cotton or flax tow, but it was not until the late 1820s that power spinning was applied successfully to the making of fine yarns from long flax fibres. A much simpler operation was the twisting of two or more handspun yarns together to make thread, but in spite of encouragement of Irish threadmakers by the Linen Board, the linen-thread trade in the eighteenth century was centred in Scotland, although much Irish yarn was used. In 1784, however, John Barbour came from Paisley to Lisburn to set up a thread works and erected machinery to twist the yarn; the works was later transferred to Hilden and in 1837 contained almost 1,000 twisting spindles. The linen-thread trade in the north of Ireland expanded rapidly, and towards the end of the nineteenth century the Linen Thread Company was formed with commercial interests all over the world, one of the first of the great monopoly combines.[9] There were also some independent local thread manufacturers, but the number of twisting spindles in the north of Ireland has remained small when compared with the total of flax spindles. Most local makers of textile machinery produced twisting frames before embarking on the more difficult spinning and preparing machines.

After flax 'line' has been hackled, a spreader or 'spreadboard' is used to form it into a continuous ribbon or sliver. The sliver is doubled and drawn out again on drawing frames, to ensure greater uniformity. It is further drawn out and given a slight twist on the roving frame, and finally spun on the spinning frame. Tow sliver from the carding machine is doubled and drawn in the same way, and also subjected to roving and spinning. Machinery had been developed in England by 1790 for spinning flax, but only coarse yarns could be produced. John Marshall of Leeds was one of the pioneers of the industry and by 1825 he had four steam-driven mills. Other firms followed Marshall's example in spinning flax by power in Leeds, and also in Lancashire and Scotland, but no attempt was made to set up flax-spinning mills in Ireland until after 1800. Consequently, Britain captured practically the whole of the coarse linen trade, and in Ireland only the fine linen trade of Ulster was unaffected.

In an effort to retrieve the situation, the Linen Board offered premiums between 1801 and 1811 for the erection of spindles powered by water, steam, horses, or oxen; the amount was at first 10s, but was eventually raised to 30s per spindle. It was a condition of payment that there should be sufficient preparing machinery to keep the spindles at work. The first Irish mill for spinning flax by power was in Cork, perhaps as early as 1803; the first power-driven flax spindles in the north of Ireland were erected in county Down in 1805. By 1809 in twelve Ulster mills 6,369 spindles had been installed, on which the Board had expended £9,619 in premiums. Progress in the power spinning of flax in the north of Ireland was slow, and one reason may have been that the low cost of handspun yarn discouraged development; there was also difficulty in obtaining efficient machinery. The equipment for John Stitt's mill at Comber in county Down was supplied and erected in 1808 by John Procter, flax and tow machine maker of Leeds, who in June of that year announced that he would remain for a few weeks at Comber and 'flattered himself he would give every satisfaction should any person favour him with their orders'. The machinery of the mill erected at Milford in county Armagh in 1808 was also supplied from Leeds, which had become the principal centre for the making of flax machinery, by reason of the early concentration of flax spinning there.[10]

Not all the machinery brought from England 'gave every satisfaction' to Irish flax spinners. Thomas Crosthwaite, one of the owners of a flax-spinning mill established in 1810 at Lucan near Dublin, gave evidence to the select committee on the Irish linen trade in 1825 to the effect that the first set of machinery which his firm obtained from England was useless and had to be broken up, while in 1825 they were obtaining improved machines and destroying the second set of equipment. He complained that the machine makers in England were so busy that they could not take on more work, and orders placed ten months before had not yet been fulfilled.[11] Those spinners who sought to have their machinery made locally did not necessarily fare any better. Josiah Bryan of Balnamore, near Ballymoney, contracted with William Booth, a Belfast machine maker, for the erection 'in a workmanlike manner' of machinery for spinning linen yarn before 25 December 1808, so that Bryan could claim the premium offered by the Linen Board. Far from being made in a workmanlike manner the machinery was so bad that Bryan had to throw out most of it, alter the rest, and get further machinery from England. Naturally he sued Booth for damages, and at the civil bill court at Carrickfergus in February 1812 was awarded £500 and costs.[12] Bryan had the additional consolation of obtaining the premium of £600 from the Linen Board for the 400 spindles he had eventually installed successfully.

If this was typical of the performance of the Belfast makers of textile machinery in the first quarter of the nineteenth century, it is no wonder that John Marshall of Leeds gave it as his opinion to the select committee on the linen trade that the people in Ireland were not skilful enough to make flax-spinning machinery, and he even doubted whether sufficiently skilful workmen could be found in Ireland to operate efficiently any machinery sent over from England. He concluded that the difficulty in procuring and managing machinery in Ireland was the chief factor hindering the establishment of more mills for spinning linen yarn.[13]

The premium of 30s per spindle offered by the Linen Board amounted to about 50 per cent of the cost of erection of spinning mills at that period. There were uncertainties in most of the Linen Board schemes which made the public chary of them, and lengthy delays in paying premiums, so that millowners had to find the original capital themselves before they could know whether, or when, their premiums would be paid. Even so, it is remarkable that the encouragement given to flax spinning by the Linen Board did not result in greater progress being made by the Belfast machine makers. The most likely explanation is the inherent difficulty encountered in producing machinery which would spin the fine counts of yarn in demand in Ulster.

Until 1820, power spinning was still confined to coarse yarn, and the fine linen trade of the north of Ireland still depended on hand-spun yarn. About that time, the system of drawing flax through gills or coarse hackles came into use; this enabled a much more uniform yarn to be produced and made possible the spinning by power of medium linen yarns. The difficulty of drawing out fine yarns had still not been solved, and some novel approach was needed, for the improvements in cotton spinning could not be applied to flax, which consists of long fibres, each made up of short ultimate fibres bound together by a gummy substance. Even with gill spinning, the flax fibres were drawn in their full length, the ultimate fibres remaining glued together. The problem was solved by the development of wet spinning. In 1825 James Kay of Preston obtained a patent for a wet spinning process in which the flax rove was steeped in cold water for five to six hours. This loosened the gummy matter and enabled the fibres to be drawn out in their elementary condition; it also involved placing the retaining and drawing rollers only a few inches apart, for the steeped rove would not hold together to be drawn out with the long reaches which had been used in dry spinning. The process made possible the spinning by machinery of virtually the whole range of linen yarns and rapidly began to drive handspun yarns off the market. Subsequently the steeping in cold water was replaced by passing the rove through a trough of hot water on the spinning frame.

A Frenchman named Philip de Girard claimed to have developed wet spinning before Kay, but his method seems to have involved only a brief damping in the preparing machinery, which could not have loosened the ultimate fibres of the flax. Kay was compelled to bring an action for the infringement of his patent and finally in the House of Lords the decision was given against him, and he had to pay heavy costs. The case was lost on a technical point over bringing the rollers close together, not because de Girard's prior invention was established, but the decision against Kay was of great importance as it gave the advantages of wet spinning to the whole linen trade immediately.[14] The new method was quickly adopted in Britain, and wet-spun yarns from Britain soon began to compete with the fine yarns still being spun by hand in Ireland. It looked as if the fine section of the Irish linen trade might be lost, as the coarse section of the industry had been when power spinning was first introduced. The Linen Board again attempted to encourage the use of the new process in Ireland, and made grants to a number of firms for the introduction of wet spinning, but the Board was dissolved in 1828, just at the time when the first wet-spinning mills were being erected in the north of Ireland without any Government assistance.

In 1827 John Hind, the son of a Manchester cotton spinner, in partnership with Thomas and Andrew Mulholland, set up experimental wet-spinning machinery at premises in Francis Street in Belfast, where they had previously had a cotton power-loom factory. When the Mulhollands' large cotton mill in York Street was burned down in 1828 it was decided to rebuild it as a linen mill, as the machinery at Francis Street had shown promise. John Hind went to England and obtained access to several of the Leeds mills, and on his return, machinery for the new York Street mill was constructed to the latest designs in a small workshop set up at MacAdam's Soho Foundry in Townsend Street. Linen spinning was a subject for industrial espionage, just as cotton spinning had been when introduced! The Francis Street mill may have been the first in the north of Ireland to use wet spinning for linen; the first to go into production on a substantial scale was probably that of James Murland at Castlewellan in county Down, established at the latest in 1828. After that, the development of wet spinning was rapid, and by 1833 ten mills were employing over 5,000 workers within a 20 mile radius of Belfast. By 1850 there were sixty-nine flax spinning mills in Ireland, sixty-three of them in Ulster. The number of flax spindles in Ireland increased rapidly over the next ten years, from some 300,000 in 1850 to nearly 600,000 in 1860.

The cotton famine resulting from the civil war in America led to a further expansion of linen production, and the number of spindles continued to increase for about ten years after the cotton shortage ended, reaching almost a million by the end of the 1870s. Too much equipment had been installed for normal output, and the number of spindles declined gradually to 844,000 by 1900.[15] Another increase in activity came before 1914, but the war, while it created a large demand for linen for aeroplane fabric, interrupted the supply of imported flax and disrupted production. Between the wars production and employment fluctuated, but showed a steady tendency to diminish with changes in fashion and competition from cheaper materials. The second world war again led to a shortage of fibre and firms in the north of Ireland were unable to supply many of their traditional markets, where linen was often replaced by other fabrics produced in the countries concerned. The large backlog of world demand for textiles had been filled by the early 1950s and the post-war boom ended.

Since then the linen industry has found it increasingly difficult to meet competition from man-made fibres and the trend in production has been generally downwards. Some linen firms have diversified

into other activities, but many have gone out of business; perhaps
the greatest shock was the closure in 1961 of the York Street flax-
spinning mill in Belfast, which, to the local makers of textile machinery, had at one time appeared to be an institution just as secure as
the Bank of England.

Apart from the rapid increase in flax spinning in the north of
Ireland in the third quarter of the nineteenth century, the Belfast
makers of textile machinery also benefited from the gradual concentration in the area of the United Kingdom flax-spinning industry.
Though mill spinning of flax commenced in Leeds it had ceased to
expand there by 1860, and even before that had begun to decline in
England as a whole. By 1890 it had almost ceased in England, and
had ceased to be a major industry in Scotland. The transfer to
Ireland was so continuous as to be almost imperceptible and it left
no important gaps, because the manufacture was replaced in Britain
by more profitable ones, such as the jute industry in eastern Scotland.[16] The north of Ireland has remained one of the main flax-
spinning regions of the world, and this has ensured that machinery
for preparing and spinning flax continued to be made in Belfast,
although the local manufacturers have had to rely on export orders
for a substantial part of their business from the last quarter of the
nineteenth century, and in recent times flax machinery has ceased to
be their main product. Like the making of hackling machinery, the
production of preparing and spinning machinery in the north of
Ireland has been confined to Belfast, not only because the linen
industry has been concentrated within a 30 mile radius of the city,
but also because the making of such machinery was too specialised
a job for the small provincial ironfounders.

John Hind and the Mulhollands were the only pioneers of the wet
spinning of flax who are recorded as having their machinery made
locally, although others may have done so. The Belfast Foundry in
Donegall Street claimed that in 1834 they were the first engineering
firm in Ireland to produce successful machinery for wet-spinning
flax. The Ordnance Survey field memoir for the parish of Carn-

money, written in 1838 or 1839, noted that the spinning mill of Bell & Calvert at Whitehouse near Belfast was then the only one in Ireland equipped with machinery wholly of Irish manufacture; the 30 hp steam engine and the spinning machinery with 5,000 spindles had been made at the Belfast Foundry. There is no evidence that spinning machinery continued to be made at MacAdam's Soho Foundry after the equipment for the York Street mill had been completed under the direction of John Hind. The firm did, of course, continue to make flax-scutching machinery.

The Belfast makers of flax-spinning machinery must have built up their reputation quickly, for by 1846 they were seen to be a serious threat to the security of their Leeds competitors. It was alleged that they had progressed by taking models of the latest machines from Leeds, Manchester, or Preston, with the aid of English workmen, but there was nothing unusual about this and indeed it was common practice in the engineering industry in Britain at the time. No matter how it has been achieved, Belfast had become the 'Leeds and Manchester' of Ireland, and whereas a few years previously all the flax-preparing and flax-spinning machinery required in the north of Ireland was made in Leeds, now the Belfast firms sent their machinery in large quantities to the 'very door of their English rivals' and also competed with them successfully in the French, Belgian, Prussian, Russian, and American markets.[17]

In 1852 the following firms were established as ironfounders and makers of flax-spinning machinery in Belfast:

	Men and boys employed
James Combe & Co—Falls Foundry	380
Samuel Boyd & Co—Belfast Foundry	250
J. Scrimgeour—Albert Street (subsequently James Mackie & Sons)	150
James Harper—Wilson Street	100
Thompson & Co—Brown's Square	90
Reynolds Brothers—McClenaghan's Court	30
Total	1,000

The figures are obviously a rough estimate, for otherwise they would hardly add up to such a convenient total.[18]

James Combe, a Scotsman, established the Falls Foundry in 1845 to supply equipment for the local railways then being built. From about 1850 the firm produced textile machinery and made a number of important contributions to its development. The name was changed to Combe, Barbour & Combe, and in 1900 the firm became part of Fairbairn Lawson Combe Barbour Ltd. The Falls Foundry continued to be the principal producer of flax-spinning machinery in Belfast until 1914, and the making of textile machinery continued until 1955, when Fairbairn Lawson Combe Barbour ceased production in Belfast. The Belfast Foundry was already well established when the demand for flax-spinning machinery arose, and it was natural that the firm should take advantage of the new market. They continued to make spinning and twisting frames up to the end of the nineteenth century, when they went out of business.

James Scrimgeour was a Scotsman who had works in Albert Street from the 1840s, where he made textile machinery, including spinning frames. Little is known about him or his products, but a number of his spinning frames were listed in the inventories of machinery to be sold in the flax-spinning mills in Belfast which went into liquidation in the 1870s, when the linen boom collapsed.

James Mackie came from Scotland to erect steam engines at a flax-spinning mill in Drogheda, and when in Ireland he accepted the post of manager at James Scrimgeour's works. He was subsequently offered a partnership, but declined and instead lent money to Scrimgeour on deposit. This proved to have been a wise decision, for when Scrimgeour failed in business the creditors were unable to establish that James Mackie was a partner and therefore liable for the debts. While James Mackie did not recover all the money he had lent to Scrimgeour, he was able to take over the Albert Street premises in 1858 with some of the machine tools and set up in business for himself. He did not immediately continue the production of spinning frames, and at first had only a small number of employees engaged in fluting rollers, turning spindles, and repairing textile machinery. After a few years the manufacture of flax cutters, bundling presses, and twisting frames commenced; later spinning frames were added, and by 1892 about a hundred wet-spinning frames were being produced each year. In the early 1890s a substantial export business had been built up, and the firm moved to much larger premises at Springfield Road; by the end of the century preparing machinery was being produced to complete the range of flax machinery. Mackies, continuing to make flax preparing and spinning machinery, began to branch out in the early 1920s into the manufacture of jute machinery, which by 1929 had become their most important product. In the pre-war period the company became leading suppliers of sisal and hard-fibre spinning machinery, and after the war developed new types of machinery for spinning synthetic fibres and wool.

James Harper was established in Wilson Street by 1843, but does not seem to have continued in business beyond the early 1860s. Thompson & Co appear in the directories only from 1839 to 1868, and in their latter years at least they seem to have specialised in winding equipment rather than in spinning machinery. The Reynolds brothers, James and Peter, served their apprenticeships in the Belfast Foundry and set up in business in McClenaghan's Court off Mill Street in Belfast about 1850, but it was not until the American civil war that they concentrated on making spinning machinery. In 1865 they were making eleven spinning frames a month. They removed to Grosvenor Street, but subsequently disagreed and for some time had two adjacent but separate establishments, James Reynolds's Linfield Foundry and Peter Reynolds's Northern Foundry, both in Grosvenor Street. Peter Reynolds went out of business in the late 1870s, but James Reynolds & Co continued to make a comprehensive range of flax-preparing and spinning machinery until 1929, although they specialised in equipment for making thread, twine, and ropes.

When the flax-spinning industry in the north of Ireland ceased to expand by the late 1860s, the local engineering firms had to develop export markets or diversify and produce equipment for other fibres, such as hemp or jute. Those which did not do so went out of business by the beginning of the present century. The three firms which continued to make flax-preparing and spinning machinery, Mackies, Reynolds, and the Falls Foundry, benefited from the expansion of flax spinning up to 1914 and from the demand for machinery to re-equip the European linen industry after the war, but the market stagnated through the post-war depressions and by the end of the 1920s Reynolds had gone out of business and Mackies were making more machinery for jute than for flax. After the second world war there was again a demand for machinery to replace what had been destroyed, and also a need for linen firms to install new equipment to keep up with the considerable technical advances made since the end of the 1930s. This demand was largely satisfied by the early 1950s, and the making of textile machinery at the Falls Foundry ceased in 1955; Mackies continued to develop machinery for other fibres, the proportion of flax equipment in their total output declining.

The flax spinners of the north of Ireland evidently took a keen interest in developments in textile machinery, for according to William Charley, writing in 1862, 'they examined carefully every new improvement and, if they approved of it, at once brought it into use in their mills'.[19] In their report for 1875, the Flax Supply Association claimed that one of the advantages the local flax spinners had over their continental competitors was 'superior skill and excellence in machinery'; but they issued a warning that there was no fixed tenure of this position, as the continental spinners were rapidly introducing the 'most modern and approved machinery',[20] much of which was made in Belfast. The close association between spinners and machine makers benefited both parties. It was said in 1874 that the Belfast machine-making establishments were 'surrounded by spinning mills and were visited almost daily by the spinners, who thus were able to see the progress being made in the execution of their orders, and to point out their exact requirements and the defects of previous machines'. This led rapidly to improvements in the construction of machinery and in the methods of using it, which 'placed the Irish spinners and makers of flax machinery in a deservedly high position in the commercial world'.[21] Many of the improvements in flax machinery since the middle of the nineteenth century originated in Belfast.

The fact that cotton machinery does not lend itself to the preparing and spinning of flax protected the Belfast textile-machine makers against competition from the makers of cotton machinery. On the other hand, the makers of flax machinery had no great difficulty in producing machinery for spinning hemp and jute, which are also bast fibres. The large complement of preparing machinery required for flax compared with cotton led to a substantial difference in the cost of mills; it was estimated that flax-spinning machinery cost four or five times as much per spindle as cotton machinery, and this was of benefit to the makers of flax machinery. One effect of the differences between cotton and flax machinery was that in the nineteenth century a flax mill required up to four times as many operatives as a cotton mill with the same number of spindles; this helped to concentrate the linen industry in Ireland where there was less competition for labour than in Britain.[22]

Linen Weaving

Although the handloom weaving of linen in the north of Ireland declined in the first half of the nineteenth century, this was not due to the introduction of power looms in the local linen industry. Handloom weavers in and around Belfast abandoned linen for cotton, and when the power weaving of coarse linen was introduced in England and Scotland in the first quarter of the century, this reduced the demand for such fabrics from Ireland. The Irish handloom weavers depended on a combination of weaving with subsistence farming, especially potato cultivation, and the potato famine of the 1840s removed this prop from their economy. They were also adversely affected by the concentration of spinning in the mills, for hand spinning in the home had provided them with a convenient supply of yarn, as well as a source of income for the female members of the family.[23] As the nineteenth century progressed the handloom weaver's position deteriorated, but in spite of this the handloom continued to be the chief means of weaving linen in the north of Ireland until after 1850. In many districts there was a weekly market for handwoven linen as late as the 1870s, and even in 1891 it could be said that around Ballymena hardly a cottage lacked its handloom, and for many families weaving was the main occupation.[24] Indeed, the handloom weaving of linen damask continued into the 1960s, but by then expensive handwoven goods were pricing themselves out of the market.

In the first half of the nineteenth century the handloom weavers were prepared to work for very low earnings and this would have reduced the advantages to be gained from investment in power looms. So long as man's labour could be had at the handloom in Ireland for 1s a day it was felt that no power loom could work much, if at all, cheaper.[25] The power looms of the mid-nineteenth century produced four times as much cloth as a handloom weaver, but this was nothing like the saving in labour of contemporary spinning machinery which enabled a girl to attend 160 spindles, each of which could do the work of two spinsters; there was therefore less incentive to mechanise weaving. The most important factor, however, in delaying the adoption of power looms in the north of Ireland was the concentration on the production of fine linen, for not until about 1850 was the power loom developed to the stage of being able to weave this type of fabric. At Dunfermline, the centre of the fine linen trade in Scotland, power looms were not used until 1849, although they had been in use in Scotland for some time on coarse linen; power looms were first used for fine linen in the north of Ireland about the same time. After 1850, the introduction of power looms was rapid, and as the earnings of handloom weavers remained low it is clear that the delay in using them in the north of Ireland was caused by technical factors rather than by the cheap labour of the handloom weavers.

Handlooms for linen were made by the groups of craftsmen who also made cotton looms, but though undertaking repairs or rebuilding, the Belfast makers of textile machinery were unable to compete successfully with the power-loom makers in Britain. The delay in the introduction of power looms in the local linen industry may have been partly responsible, although the delay in the adoption of power spinning did not prevent Belfast firms making flax-spinning machinery. There was much less 'making' in a loom than in preparing or spinning machinery, and therefore less margin for profit. What is more important, there was less difference between linen and cotton looms than between flax and cotton spinning machinery. English loom makers had, therefore, no great difficulty in producing linen looms and, after the delay in adopting power looms in the north of Ireland, the local makers of textile machinery would have found it very difficult to begin loom making in competition with them.

Some local inventors turned their attention to the Jacquard mechanisms attached to the hand or power loom for weaving linen damask. In 1869 the 'Bessbrook machine' was invented by Henry Barcroft of the Bessbrook Spinning Company; this was claimed to be the first automatic twilling Jacquard machine, and to give scope for greater richness of designs in cloth of finer qualities than had previously been possible. About 1880 George Benson began to make his improved Jacquard machines at Durham Street in Belfast, but it is not clear how long he continued to do so. Other firms have continued to make Jacquard mechanisms, and this has been the only type of equipment used directly in weaving linen to be made in the north of Ireland, other than reeds, heddles, shuttles, and other small parts for looms. Some of the local engineering firms made machinery for preparing yarn for weaving, and from the eighteenth century equipment has been made for bleaching and finishing the cloth.

Linen Bleaching and Finishing

The first sections of the linen industry to which power-driven machinery was applied were bleaching and finishing. Water-powered machines for washing and rubbing the cloth, and 'beetling engines' for finishing it were introduced by the second quarter of the eighteenth century. The wash mills were derived from the tuck mills, which had long been used for finishing woollen cloth, but the beetling process was peculiar to linen. The cloth was wrapped round a wooden cylinder which revolved slowly while a row of wooden 'beetles' were allowed to fall on it repeatedly; after some time this produced a highly glazed finish on the linen. These mills were attached to bleachgreens, which required plenty of land for laying out the cloth during bleaching, and water for washing as well as for power; they were, therefore, situated in the countryside. The making of bleaching and finishing machinery was first a job for the itinerant millwrights, and later mainly for the provincial engineering firms, the principal centres being Banbridge, Bessbrook, Larne, and Portadown. In Belfast, bleaching and finishing machinery was not made by the firms which made spinning machinery, but some half-dozen of the local engineering firms made beetling engines, mangles, calenders, and other bleaching equipment. There was a substantial decrease in the number of bleachgreens in the north of Ireland in the first half of the nineteenth century, but this was accompanied by an increase in their size, and did not necessarily result in a decline in business for the firms supplying bleaching machinery. After 1850, however, there was serious competition from firms in Britain which had developed improved machinery for bleaching, dyeing, and finishing cotton, which was also suitable for linen. Only the beetling process was peculiar to linen, and in the making of beetling engines the local firms had little competition from outside the north of Ireland.

When machinery was being introduced for textile printing in

Page 71   (above) *Chambers car built in 1906;* (below) *Straddle carrier produced by subsidiary of Short Brothers & Harland Ltd*

Page 72   (above) *5 ft 3 in gauge 2-6-0 Mogul class locomotive 'King Edward VIII' built York R
1937; (below) Diesel shunting locomotive built by Harland & Wolff for LMS (NCC) 193*

Britain in the last quarter of the eighteenth century, the Irish printers reacted by calling on the government for further protection, not by using machinery themselves, and it was not until the beginning of the nineteenth century that machinery was used in the print works in the north of Ireland. The number of textile-printing works decreased with the decline of the cotton industry, but there are still some half-dozen firms engaged in printing mainly cotton and linen. The delay in the introduction of machinery in the north of Ireland enabled the machine makers in Britain to establish themselves as suppliers of textile-printing equipment in the area, and the few local firms which attempted to compete were not successful, although at the peak of the trade in the first half of the nineteenth century large numbers were employed locally to engrave the copper plates or rollers for the printing machines.[26]

Other Textiles

The woollen industry in the north of Ireland was not extensive enough to justify local engineering firms developing machinery for it in the nineteenth century, and it was not until after the second world war that Mackies began to make worsted-spinning machinery. Machinery has been made for some fibres which are akin to flax, even though most of it was for customers in Britain and overseas.

Hemp was grown in Ireland at the beginning of the eighteenth century. The Irish Linen Board was supposed to encourage its production and improve the methods of processing it; indeed the full title of the Board was the 'Trustees of the linen and hempen manufactures of Ireland'. The Board did not have much success, however, and nearly all the fibre used in Ireland was imported, in spite of sporadic attempts by the Board to revive its cultivation. Some hemp was used for making canvas, but its chief use was for cordage. In the first half of the nineteenth century, there were about a dozen small ropewalks in operation in Belfast, and another dozen in the provincial towns of Ulster, but the number of small firms

E

declined after the formation, in 1876, of the Belfast Ropework Company, which expanded to become the largest single ropeworks in the world. The demand at first was for ropes for rigging ships which came to Belfast in the course of trade or for overhaul, and also for Belfast-built sailing vessels and the early full-rigged steamers. The Belfast Ropework Company later exploited the increasing use of reaping machinery by producing binder twines, and also made trawl twines, nets, and a large variety of cords. At first, the ropeworks imported machines from America; later they undertook development work on ropemaking machinery, producing the designs and the patterns for the castings to be made in local foundries, and then carried out the machining and erection themselves. The making of rope and cordage machinery gradually became a job for the specialist, and the company gave up this type of work.

Machinery for hackling hemp was made by the firms which made flax-hackling machines, and rope and cordage machinery was made at the Falls Foundry, by James Reynolds & Co at their Linfield Foundry, and later by James Mackie & Sons; but by the 1960s Mackies were the only makers still in production, and cordage machinery was only a small fraction of their total output. The increasing use of hard fibres obtained from the leaves of certain plants such as sisal for cordage and other purposes led to the making of preparing and spinning machinery in Belfast. Before the second world war, Mackies began to improve this equipment, and after the war they rapidly became the major world suppliers of hard-fibre machinery.

The problems in preparing and spinning jute are similar to those encountered in the dry spinning of flax. This helps to explain the making of jute machinery in Belfast in the nineteenth century, in spite of the small extent of the jute industry in Ireland. Until the 1920s, Belfast was not a major supplier of jute machinery, but in later years, in spite of the fact that Fairbairn Lawson Combe Barbour did not make jute machinery at the Falls Foundry, Belfast overtook many of the other centres, following the increased output of jute equipment by Mackies. This resulted from the development by the company of a complete range of jute machinery, including looms, which greatly increased mill productivity. Felt making was also associated with the linen industry, for the first type of felt made in Belfast was sheathing felt for ships, made from waste flax fibres impregnated with pitch and tar. Ritchie Hart & Co of Belfast made felt-making machinery, and their interest in this type of equipment arose from the fact that the Ritchies were felt makers.

It was found that rayon staple could be spun successfully on flax spindles and woven on linen looms, and in recent years rayon has accounted for up to 30 per cent of the output of the linen firms in the north of Ireland. Since the second world war, the region has become a major producer of synthetic fibres, and these have been used increasingly by local makers of cordage, yarn, and thread; a substantial market for synthetic-fibre machinery has also arisen in Great Britain and overseas. Mackies have developed equipment for carding, preparing, spinning, twisting, and winding man-made fibres, and the production of this type of machinery has expanded as the demand for machinery for natural fibres has declined.

It might have been expected that the expansion of the making-up trades, especially shirtmaking, would have resulted in the production of sewing machines in the north of Ireland, but this does not appear to have happened. George Benson of Belfast patented a hemstitch machine in 1879,[27] and in 1888 he formed Benson's Patent Hemstitching Machine Company, which soon afterwards claimed to be the largest makers of hemstitch machines and to have five models on the market, but it seems doubtful whether the machines were made in Belfast. A number of other local men contributed to the development of sewing machines, but were not able to market models of their own. The most likely explanation is that at that time the north of Ireland lacked the experience in light, precision, repetitive metalworking, necessary for making sewing machines at prices competitive with those from Britain and America. The sewing machine was the first major consumer appliance, and the limited local market would also have placed local manufacturers at a disadvantage. The engineering firms in Londonderry were able to benefit from the concentration of shirtmaking in the city through selling equipmentspecially designed to speed up the making of shirts.

Textile machinery was the first type of equipment which engineering firms in the north of Ireland themselves improved and developed. They worked in close co-operation with their customers, and the local textile producers were also keenly interested in technical developments; both benefited from the work of the Linen Industry Research Association. James Mackie & Sons were pioneers of the package-deal arrangement whereby the machinery manufacturer takes responsibility for the planning, supply, and installation of equipment, and also the starting up of textile production. In modern jargon this means selling 'software' as well as 'hardware'. As a result of this co-operation with customers, both at home and overseas, many significant improvements in the design of textile machinery for flax, hemp, jute, hard fibres and synthetics have originated in the north of Ireland. Although from the 1960s there was only one large firm making a full range of machinery, some dozen smaller firms undertook repairs and renovations, or the supplying of specialised equipment or spare parts. It would not be true to say that the textile-machinery industry in the north of Ireland had contracted since the mid-nineteenth century, for Mackies now produce a much wider range of machinery than was available in the area in the past, and their output is probably greater than the total previously produced by a larger number of firms; in addition, the company were employing over 6,000 people in the 1960s, more than were employed at any time in the past in making textile machinery in the north of Ireland. Mackies have indeed risen to a dominant position in the supply of flax, jute, and hard-fibre machinery, and have become major suppliers of machinery to spin and weave man-made fibres. The company make a substantial contribution to the exports of Northern Ireland, for over 80 per cent of the machinery produced is for customers outside the United Kingdom.

CHAPTER SIX

Marine Engineering

IN the north of Ireland, the manufacture of engines for the propulsion of ships developed later than the making of land engines, but eventually it became a more important and technically a more advanced section of the engineering industry. Walter H. Wilson, a partner in Harland & Wolff, pointed out in 1891 that few engines in local mills exceeded 2,000 ihp, but engines six to eight times as powerful were not then unusual in ships. Mill engines ran for less than ten hours each day, with stops at breakfast and lunch times, while in crossing the Atlantic marine engines ran at full power nonstop for six to ten days. A voyage to Australia or New Zealand meant up to 1,200 hours continuous running, the equivalent of half a year's work for a land engine. Marine engines had no solid foundations and every ton of superfluous metal raised the shipowners' running costs. A higher standard of design was therefore required than for land engines, and it is no wonder that Wilson regarded marine engineering as the superior science.[1]

Wooden Ships

Wooden sailing vessels were built at various suitable places round the coast of the north of Ireland before 1800. Mostly they were small, requiring no elaborate plant or equipment for their construction, and the trade was not extensive because supplies of suitable timber were no longer plentiful in Ireland by the eighteenth century. Belfast was not then an important shipbuilding centre, and it was not until 1791 that William Ritchie transferred his business from Saltcoats in Ayrshire, and established a permanent shipbuilding yard on the Lagan. In the first half of the nineteenth century, three firms built wooden sailing vessels in Belfast: Ritchie & Mac-Laine, Thompson & Kirwan, and Charles Connell & Sons. But from 1820 to 1850 only about fifty vessels were built. None of these firms attempted to make marine engines; the engines for the few wooden steamers which were constructed in Belfast were supplied by Victor Coates & Co. One of the first steamships built in Ireland was the *Belfast*, launched in 1820 by Ritchie & MacLaine with engines of 70 hp by Victor Coates. In 1838, Charles Connell & Sons launched the *Aurora*, with Coates engines of 230 hp; this was claimed to be the largest ship built in Ireland up to that time.[2]

Belfast was not the place where steamships were first constructed in Ireland. The first steamer built in Ireland appears to have been the *City of Cork*, completed by Andrew and Michael Hennessy of Passage in 1816; her 12 hp engines were supplied by Boulton & Watt. In 1817 they built the *Waterloo*, and the engines were on this occasion made in Cork; this was claimed to be the first steamship completely fitted out in Ireland.[3] In the first half of the nineteenth century Cork was a much more important shipbuilding centre than Belfast. Dublin, Drogheda, and Waterford also produced some wooden steamers, and in Londonderry Captain William Coppin launched one of the first screw steamers in 1843. He built the engines and boilers as well as the hull.

Iron Sailing Ships

Belfast was not at a disadvantage in the second half of the nineteenth century through having lagged behind in wooden shipbuilding. The building of iron ships was not a further extension of wooden shipbuilding, but a different craft, a development of boilermaking. Thus, the first iron vessel launched in Belfast was constructed, not in one of the existing shipbuilding yards, but by the engineering and boilermaking firm of Victor Coates & Co. This was the *Countess of Caledon*, an iron steamer of 30 hp launched in 1838 and used for towing lighters on Lough Neagh. Iron shipbuilding

continued on a small scale in the 1840s, and there was little evidence
to justify the optimistic forecast, made by the *Belfast Peoples' Magazine* in 1847, that iron shipbuilding was likely to become 'a permanent and profitable channel of industrial enterprise in Belfast, employing a large number of workmen'.[4]

It was not until 1853 that a second firm undertook iron shipbuilding on the Lagan; in that year the Belfast Harbour Commissioners laid out a yard on the Queen's Island for Robert Hickson, a partner in the Eliza Street ironworks in Belfast, but the yard did not begin to prosper until it was taken over by Hickson's manager, E. J. Harland, in 1858. Victor Coates gave up shipbuilding in the 1860s, but in 1868 MacIlwaine & Lewis began ship repairing at the Abercorn Basin, and in the 1870s branched out into shipbuilding. Later, in 1880, the other firm of Belfast shipbuilders, Workman Clark & Co, laid their first keel.

Although some iron steamships were built in the first half of the nineteenth century, it was not until the 1880s that the iron or steel steamer became the dominant form of ocean transport. The early steamers carried passengers and mails successfully, but their engines were so inefficient that fuel costs were high, and coal took up a large proportion of the space on board. They could not be used economically for the transport of bulky cargoes such as grain. There was delay in the adoption of iron even for sailing ships, for the fouling of iron hulls on long voyages reduced speed and coppered wooden ships were faster; good, uniform iron was difficult to produce, and steel was not competitive with iron until the late 1880s. The great advantage of iron over wood as a shipbuilding material was its greater strength, which permitted a reduction in thickness, making an iron ship lighter than a wooden one of similar dimensions. More important, it enabled larger vessels to be constructed; wooden ships had been limited in practice to about 300 ft in length, but there was practically no limit to the length of iron ships. There was, however, a serious problem in handling spars and sails of abnormal dimensions, and sailing vessels over 2,000 tons were unusual. The scientific study of winds and currents resulted in a reduction in the duration of voyages in the second half of the nineteenth century, and this prolonged the period during which the sailing ship could compete successfully with the steamer.[5] For a time iron, and later steel, sailing vessels were favoured by shipowners, and a substantial number were built in the north of Ireland. Iron sailing ships were constructed at Robert Hickson's shipyard on the Queen's Island from 1853 until the yard was taken over by E. J. Harland in 1858. Harland & Wolff concentrated on steamships, but they also built some sailing vessels, and in 1890 completed the last sailing ship for the White Star Line, the steel four-masted barque *California* of over 3,000 gross tons. Large sailing vessels were also built in Belfast by Workman Clark, and smaller ones by MacIlwaine & MacColl. It is not clear whether the sailing ships built at Londonderry in the 1830s and 1840s were of wood or iron, but iron ships were built there from 1882 to 1892. From 1874 to 1893, sailing vessels were constructed at Carrickfergus, at first in wood, and later in iron and steel. The hulls for two steamships were also made here. Ship and boat building was also carried out on a small scale at Larne and other ports in the north of Ireland, and on the inland waterways; in latter years mainly fishing and pleasure craft were produced.[6] An iron or steel shipyard required expensive machinery and equipment, even for sailing vessels, so shipbuilding became concentrated in the few yards with the necessary capital. Marine engineering demanded further costly plant, including a foundry, and only the larger shipbuilding firms made their own engines. In the north of Ireland this meant the concentration of marine engine building in Belfast.

Steamships

Iron ships developed slowly, but improving the efficiency of marine engines took longer still, and in 1850 steam vessels accounted for less than 5 per cent of the total tonnage of the United Kingdom. The marine engines of the period were of the single-expansion type using low-pressure steam; coal consumption was high and there had been no significant improvement in efficiency since they were first introduced. With the development of compound engines, and screw propulsion in place of paddle wheels, the position changed rapidly; between 1863 and 1872 fuel consumption fell by 50 per cent, and so cargo space was greatly increased while fuel costs were halved. In 1882, for the first time the tonnage of new steam vessels equalled the tonnage of new sailing vessels, and from then on the proportion of steamships increased rapidly. The competitive position of the steamship improved further in the 1880s with the substitution of steel for iron hulls, and the introduction of triple-expansion engines, forced draught, and improvements in boilers, condensers, steering gear, and auxiliary equipment. In the 1890s quadruple-expansion engines were developed, and at the beginning of the twentieth century the steam turbine revolutionised high-speed traffic. After 1910 geared turbines were devised for lower speeds, and internal combustion engines began to be used in ships. As the century progressed the marine diesel engine gradually replaced the reciprocating steam engine, but the steam turbine with oil fired water-tube boilers continued to be used, especially for higher powers; occasionally turbo-electric or diesel-electric propulsion was employed. After the second world war, gas turbines were found to have advantages as marine engines for certain purposes, especially in naval vessels. From the middle of the nineteenth to the middle of the twentieth century it was generally held to be desirable to build a ship and its engines as a unit and almost all the large shipbuilding firms made their own engines, but by the 1960s it was becoming clear that specialised marine engine works not attached to shipyards might be more suited to the future pattern of marine engineering.

Harland & Wolff

E. J. Harland's first order after taking over Hickson's shipyard on the Queen's Island was for three iron screw steamers for the Liver-

pool firm of J. Bibby Sons & Co; the engines were supplied by
Macnab & Co of Greenock, and it was not until 1880 that Harland
& Wolff established their own engine works. Harland & Wolff
quickly earned a reputation by building unconventional ships; the
steamers for Bibby's marked a revolution in naval architecture. The
hulls were of iron, but they also had iron decks which greatly increased their strength. The flat bottom and square bilge produced
the characteristic 'Belfast bottom' with its greater carrying capacity.
The ships were built much longer in proportion to their beam than
was customary at the time, and a further increase in capacity was
obtained without a proportionate increase in engine power.[7] The
other series of ships which established the reputation of Harland &
Wolff was for the White Star Line, also of Liverpool. The first of
them was launched in 1870, and the company continued to have all
its ships built by Harland & Wolff up to 1934, when it was merged
with the Cunard Company. The first *Oceanic*, in 1870, created even
more of a sensation than the Bibby ships. Compound engines were
fitted and record-breaking speeds were achieved with drastic re-
ductions in fuel consumption. The first-class accommodation was
located amidships where the effects of motion at sea were least
noticeable, away from the vibration of the propellors, and there was
a great advance in the standard of accommodation provided. The
ship was the first of the modern type of ocean liner. Though it was
claimed that T. H. Ismay of the White Star Line suggested moving
the first-class accommodation amidships,[8] there is no doubt that the
revolutionary design as a whole was the product of the ingenuity of
Harland & Wolff. The Queen's Island shipyard made the White
Star Line, just as the White Star ships firmly established the reputation of Harland & Wolff as shipbuilders.[9] Close technical co-operation with customers was maintained, and Harland & Wolff continued to specialise in large passenger liners through the changes of
fashion in their construction, until the market declined in the early
1960s, through the capture by the airlines of a substantial proportion
of the passenger traffic across the oceans. The company built other

types of special purpose ships such as cruisers, aircraft carriers, and smaller naval vessels, cargo liners, bulk carriers, and oil tankers, rather than ordinary tramp steamers.[10]

The pioneering work of Harland & Wolff in shipbuilding is fairly well known; their activities as marine engineers are less familiar. When their engine works was established in 1880, four-cylinder tandem compound engines were in fashion. Triple-expansion engines were built from 1885, and while these marked a considerable improvement, the differing weights of the three pistons could produce unpleasant vibrations. This problem was solved by using four cylinders, either quadruple-expansion, or triple-expansion with the low-pressure cylinder divided into two, and the moving weights balanced to minimise vibration. In the 1890s large Harland & Wolff ships were powered by pairs of balanced reciprocating engines; in the first decade of the twentieth century a third screw was added, driven by a low-pressure turbine using the exhaust steam from the reciprocating engines.[11] From the late 1880s the company made engines not only for their own ships but also for cruisers and battleships built elsewhere, an indication that they had established a sound reputation. Low-pressure turbines were built first by Harland & Wolff at their works on the Clyde, and were not made at Belfast until 1912. Single reduction geared turbines were built at Belfast from 1918, and double reduction geared turbines from the early 1920s. In spite of increasing competition from diesel engines after the 1920s, steam turbines continued to be built, especially for very large ships, but reciprocating steam engines went out of fashion as main engines in the 1930s. Harland & Wolff were associated with Burmeister & Wain of Copenhagen in the establishment of works at Finnieston, Glasgow, in 1912 to produce marine diesel engines. The outbreak of war led to the Finnieston works becoming the property of Harland & Wolff, and the company continued the manufacture of diesel engines on the Clyde until 1965. The construction of main diesel engines was commenced at Belfast in the mid-1920s, and these were used increasingly for large passenger liners as well as for cargo ships. The Burmeister & Wain type became the most popular, and Harland & Wolff benefited from being the principal United Kingdom makers. The engine works at Belfast, producing both diesels and steam turbines, became one of the leading marine engineering establishments in the United Kingdom, and maintained a high level of output until the demand for marine engines declined in the late 1960s.

MacIlwaine & MacColl

In 1868, MacIlwaine & Lewis established their 'Ulster Iron Works' at the Abercorn Basin in Belfast and undertook ship repairing and general engineering. In 1876 they constructed the *Elizabeth Jane* for the Lagan canal company, the first steam screw tug boat to be built in Ireland. The firm made iron barges for the Lagan canal, and built a number of small steamers, including four for the Cork Blackrock & Passage railway company. In 1885 the firm became MacIlwaine & MacColl, and in the following year took over a new shipyard on the Queen's Island. The new firm built fifty-eight vessels between 1885 and 1893, the largest of over 5,000 tons displacement. They constructed engines for their own ships, triple-expansion engines up to 1,500 ihp, and in addition undertook the reboilering and compounding of existing steamers; they also made engines for some ships built at other Irish ports. Though they did build mainly small ships, they had facilities for building ships of the same size as those produced by Workman Clark up to the early 1890s. The shipyard and engine works were taken over by Workman Clark in 1893; one of the principals continued in business on the Queen's Road until the 1920s, undertaking mainly ship repairs, but also constructing marine engines up to 750 ihp in the first decade of the century.[12]

Workman Clark

Workman, Clark & Co laid the first keel in their 'Belfast Shipyard' on the north bank of the Lagan in 1880. In the early years, engines and boilers were obtained from the Clyde, for it was not until 1891 that they commenced building their own. Their shipyard was often referred to in Belfast as the 'wee yard', but it would not have been regarded as small if it had not been overshadowed by Harland & Wolff's mammoth undertaking. From 1900 Workman Clark were usually in the top half-dozen shipbuilders in the United Kingdom, as measured by output, and occasionally produced a greater tonnage than Harland & Wolff.

Progress was slow in the first few years, but in 1882 the company secured an order from the City Line of Glasgow, which led to the building of a long series for the company, and soon other companies became regular customers of Workman Clark. A wide variety of ships was produced, from sailing vessels and small paddle steamers to first-class passenger liners. In the early years of the twentieth century, the company pioneered several types of special-purpose ships, including the frozen meat carrier and the insulated and re-frigerated fruit carrier. Repeat orders for these special ships made Workman Clark one of the principal United Kingdom builders of cargo liners and refrigerated ships.

Output expanded steadily until 1919, but thereafter the company was beset by financial difficulties which were not solved by a change in ownership in 1920, and which grew worse during the post-war slump in shipbuilding. In 1926 the company went into liquidation, and when the property was put up for sale it was purchased by a new company, Workman, Clark (1928) Ltd, under the leadership of William Strachan, a director and secretary of the original company. The new owners succeeded in obtaining orders, especially from previous customers, but after the delivery of the tanker *Acavus* in January 1935 the yard was without work. It was purchased by National Shipbuilders Security Ltd, which had been formed in 1930 to acquire and close down redundant shipyards, in an attempt to eliminate the large excess capacity in the shipbuilding industry. Subsequently the engine works and the shipyard on the south bank of the Lagan were purchased by Harland & Wolff, but the yards on the north bank were dismantled.

As marine engineers Workman Clark made a considerable impact on the shipbuilding world. They built triple and quadruple-expansion steam engines, some linked with exhaust turbines, and early in the twentieth century obtained a licence to build Parsons steam turbines. In 1905 they had one of their major triumphs. This was the completion of the 20 knot 10,750 ton Allen liner *Victorian*, the first turbine-driven mail steamer on the Atlantic. In 1921 they constructed the first British built vessel with turbo-electric propelling machinery, and subsequently built a number of other ships with this type of propulsion, in association with the British Thomson Houston Company or Metropolitan Vickers. Some of their ships were fitted with Doxford diesel engines, but from the late 1920s the company built Sulzer marine diesel engines. The main engine works had been built on the south side of the river, where Workman Clark also leased additional shipbuilding space. When the adjacent Abercorn Engine Works of MacIlwaine & MacColl was taken over in 1893 it was modernised and used mainly for repairs and special jobs, and for making auxiliary machinery such as pumps, winches, and electric lighting sets. Most of the iron castings for the engine works were produced at the company's Cyclops Foundry at Whiteinch, Glasgow. From 1880 to 1935 Workman Clark built some 530 ships, and it was the general opinion in Belfast that if they had been able to remain in business for a few more years, the renewed demand for ships would have secured the survival of the company for at least another thirty years.[13]

Other Firms

One or two other firms in Belfast claimed to be marine engineers, but they engaged in repair work rather than the building of new engines. An exception was John Butler, who had his works on the site of the old manor mill in Millfield; in the 1880s he built two sets of triple-expansion engines for small steamers constructed at Carrickfergus. Captain William Coppin built the engines for the screw steamer *Great Northern* which he launched at Londonderry in 1843, and his foundry and engine works continued in operation for twenty-four years after he stopped building ships in 1846. Engines were not made by the later Londonderry shipbuilders who constructed steamships between 1882 and 1924, or at the smaller shipbuilding yards at Larne and elsewhere in the north of Ireland. Although Victor Coates & Co had been pioneer builders of marine engines in Belfast, the local shipbuilders did not come to rely on the Lagan Foundry in the second half of the nineteenth century, but obtained their engines from the Clyde or Thames and eventually built engine works of their own. From the very beginning E. J. Harland produced unconventional ships and so required well-designed engines, which, if not built by his own firm, could be ordered with confidence only from the specialist marine engine builders. By the last quarter of the nineteenth century, firms of general engineers such as Coates would have found it difficult to design and build large marine engines in successful competition with specialists in what was then a rapidly progressing section of the engineering industry. By that time marine engineering formed only a small part of Victor Coates's activities, although ship repairing and marine boilermaking continued until the firm closed in 1905. Many of the local engineering firms undertook work for the shipyards from time to time, and some of them produced special equipment for ships such as marine engine governors, boiler feed pumps, davits, and winches.

Ship Repairing

In the nineteenth century, ship repairing was regarded as more of a nuisance than a source of profit to large shipyards. Little ordinary repair work was undertaken by Harland & Wolff in their early years, but they did carry out what might better be termed 'ship surgery', major reconstructions of damaged vessels, and the cutting in two of steamships so that extra midships sections could be added to increase the capacity. When Lord Pirrie was in control, it was the policy of Harland & Wolff to remove repair work as far as possible from Belfast,[14] and this side of the business was concentrated at the Southampton, London, and Liverpool yards of the company, at the principal liner terminals. In later years some repair work was undertaken by Harland & Wolff at Belfast, and both Workman Clark and MacIlwaine & MacColl were anxious to secure repair contracts, but the ordinary repair work associated with the port of Belfast was carried out by two or three specialist ship repair firms. At the other ports in the north of Ireland ship repairs were carried out by the smaller shipyards, where these existed, or by the local engineering firms, but the amount undertaken in the area was small in relation to new construction. During both world wars the north of Ireland became an important centre for the repair of both naval and merchant vessels, and repair facilities at Belfast and Londonderry were greatly extended.

Boilermaking

The boilers made up to the beginning of the nineteenth century in the north of Ireland were of cast iron or copper, and were used in linen bleaching, distilling, and other processes which operated at atmospheric pressure. When boilers for steam engines began to be made locally, higher working pressures had been introduced and these continued to increase from time to time; much stronger boilers were needed, constructed of wrought iron and later of steel. The makers of steam engines set up boiler shops, and there were also a few independent boilermaking firms, for boilers had to be replaced more frequently than engines, and were used for many purposes in addition to raising steam for power.

With the decline in the making of land engines, large-scale boilermaking became concentrated in the marine engineering works, while the small boilermaking firms undertook a variety of steel fabrication

e 89   (above) *Diesel-electric train built by Ulster Transport Authority;* (below) *Bus building at UTA workshops, Belfast*

Page 90   (above) *Harry Ferguson posing in his monoplane;* (below) *Short Sunderland flying b*

work. Although MacIlwaine & Lewis patented a boiler in 1876 it was not for marine use, and in the north of Ireland no advances were made in boilermaking comparable with those in shipbuilding or marine engineering.

Growth of Shipbuilding

The expansion of shipbuilding in the north of Ireland did not begin until the second half of the nineteenth century. The period of rapid growth dates from the late 1880s, when the steel steamship had become the dominant form of ocean transport, and was brought about by the expansion in world shipping. From just over 1,000 tons in 1850, and less than 14,000 tons in 1880, output had reached 100,000 gross tons per annum in the 1890s, and 150,000 tons per annum in the first decade of the twentieth century. In 1911 a record of 184,600 tons was set, which was not equalled until 1960, and not surpassed until 1967. During the first world war the shipyards were kept busy, and after the war there was a brisk demand for ships to replace tonnage lost, but the amount of shipping constructed was far in excess of what was required, especially after the slump in world trade set in. In spite of the difficulties, the output of the shipyards in the north of Ireland continued at a fairly high level, usually over 100,000 tons per annum, throughout the 1920s and reached a peak of 168,600 tons in 1930. Output was halved in 1931, and in 1932 and 1933 Harland & Wolff launched no ships at Belfast, while the output of Workman Clark was only 6,000 tons in 1932 and 14,000 tons in 1933.

The slump led to the abandonment of many ambitious shipbuilding projects, including the proposed 1,000 ft long White Star passenger liner *Oceanic III*, the keel for which was laid by Harland & Wolff in 1928. The vessel was to have had diesel-electric drive, with forty-seven diesel engines producing 200,000 shp and giving a speed of 25 knots; at 60,000 tons it would have been the biggest ship in the world, and was estimated to cost some £3,500,000 to

F

build.[15] By the end of the 1920s it had become obvious that the capacity of the British shipbuilding industry was far in excess of the likely future demand for new ships, and that it would be necessary to eliminate a substantial proportion of the redundant capacity, to reduce the burden of fixed charges and enable the remaining yards to compete on better terms with foreign shipbuilders. This was achieved largely through the activities of National Shipbuilders Security Ltd, formed in 1930 with the support of the great majority of British shipbuilding firms and with the co-operation of the banks. The company had no compulsory powers of purchase, but gave firms in difficulties the opportunity to abandon their business at less cost to themselves and to the industry than otherwise would have been possible.

During the 1930s the capacity of the shipbuilding industry was reduced by about one-third, and the reduction was spread fairly evenly over the main shipbuilding centres. Belfast's loss through the closing of Workman Clark's yards was no worse than that suffered on the Clyde, the Tyne, the Wear, and the Tees. Belfast had one advantage over other United Kingdom shipbuilding centres in the 1930s, for when the British Government withdrew its help from the shipbuilding industry under the Trade Facilities Acts, the Government of Northern Ireland continued to give financial assistance under the corresponding Loans Guarantee Acts. This not only enabled the Union-Castle and Royal Mail lines to rebuild their fleets, but also helped to keep Harland & Wolff in business through the slump in shipbuilding. After 1935, the progress of shipbuilding in the north of Ireland depended on the success of one firm, Harland & Wolff, but in spite of the closure of Workman Clark and the other smaller shipyards, output was soon back to levels higher than were common when there were three shipyards in Belfast, and others in production elsewhere in the north of Ireland.

After 1934, shipbuilding expanded slowly, and was soon helped by the rearmament programme. From September 1939 to August 1945, over 170 warships were built at Belfast, including aircraft carriers, cruisers, frigates, minesweepers, corvettes, and landing craft, but during the war Harland & Wolff also produced some 10 per cent of the United Kingdom output of merchant ships. After the war there was a heavy demand for new mercantile tonnage, and although output was restricted by the shortage of steel, wartime losses had largely been replaced by 1950. The anticipated slackening off in demand did not materialise, owing to the Korean war, which raised freight rates, and through the continuing heavy demand for tankers. In the early 1960s the market for new ships did contract, and as the United Kingdom's share of world output had been reduced sharply since the post-war years, shipbuilding capacity was found to be in excess of the demand for new vessels. This led to a number of amalgamations, and to the closure of some shipyards, including in 1963 the Govan yard of Harland & Wolff. The position of Harland & Wolff was made worse by the virtual disappearance of demand for new passenger liners, and by the reduction in naval construction. As with other shipbuilding firms, it transpired that some orders which had been secured in the face of severe competition could be completed only at a loss. During 1966 a financial crisis developed which seemed to threaten the continued existence of the company, but as in the 1930s, the Northern Ireland Government came to its assistance by guaranteeing loans to tide the company over the difficult period. Although considerable progress had already been made in modernising the shipyards, helped by agreements with the trade unions to increase flexibility in the use of manpower, further plans were made to reduce losses and to restore shipbuilding to a profitable basis. Future prospects for Harland & Wolff were improved not only by the new dry dock at Belfast capable of handling ships of up to 200,000 tons, but also by the decision to construct a building dock where vessels up to 1,000,000 tons could be built, or two 250,000 ton tankers simultaneously. Building docks have become necessary with the increasing size of ships, for very large vessels could be damaged if launched from conventional slipways. Harland & Wolff have already secured a foothold in the market for mammoth tankers and large bulk carriers, but such ships do not provide as much employment in their construction as passenger ships, naval vessels, or cargo liners. Although the rate at which orders were placed with British shipyards began to increase in 1967, it seems likely that shipbuilding at Belfast will not employ labour on the same scale as in the past. In future the labour force may be counted in thousands rather than in tens of thousands.

The shipbuilding industry did not develop to any great extent at any centre in the north of Ireland outside Belfast. Even at the peak of their production, the shipyards at Larne, Londonderry, and the other ports, did not account for more than 5 per cent of the output of the area. Belfast had two of the largest shipyards, but that did not make the Lagan the chief shipbuilding centre of the United Kingdom. Both Harland & Wolff and Workman Clark often produced more tonnage than the principal Clyde shipyards, but the greater number of establishments on the Clyde made it by far the most important shipbuilding river. The position changed from year to year, but Belfast output was usually less than that of the Clyde and Tyne, and on a par with the Wear and Tees.

It has been suggested that the development of shipbuilding at Belfast was favoured by its proximity to Liverpool.[16] It is true that Belfast soon did become the 'shipyard of the Mersey', but it should have been no more expensive for Liverpool owners to obtain their ships from the Clyde, if suitable vessels had been available. The Mersey is nearer to Dublin than to Belfast, but that did not encourage Liverpool shipowners to place orders in Dublin. Liverpool owners were attracted to Belfast because the local shipbuilders were prepared to produce ships specially designed for their needs. The success of the Belfast firms in retaining their original customers, and rapidly adding new ones, was not based on proximity to Liverpool, or even on family ties with some of the shipowners, but on building up a group of satisfied customers who were prepared to give repeat orders, and on producing ships which drew favourable comment in the shipping trade and so encouraged owners throughout Britain and overseas to entrust orders to the Belfast shipyards. Specialisation in the building of passenger ships, cargo liners, and more recently large tankers, protected the Belfast shipbuilders against the violent fluctuations in demand which characterised the market for tramp steamers. The passenger lines and the owners of special-purpose ships tended to plan far ahead, and this produced a fairly steady demand for ships. Harland & Wolff were specialists from the beginning, and Workman Clark became specialists about 1900, but MacIlwaine & MacColl were not, and this was probably one reason why they were driven out of business, as were the other small unspecialised shipyards in the north of Ireland. The boatbuilders had something different to offer, and they were able to continue making fishing vessels and pleasure craft.

One factor which did encourage the expansion of shipbuilding at Belfast was the availability of suitable sites and good dry dock facilities. The narrow and winding channel which originally linked Belfast with the sea prevented large vessels berthing at the port until improvements were undertaken. Indeed, the poor approaches to Belfast had enabled Carrickfergus to maintain its position as the chief port on the Belfast Lough up to the end of the eighteenth century. In 1841, the Harbour Commissioners began cutting a new straight channel; the material excavated during the first stage formed an island on the county Down side of the river, which was called 'Dargan's Island' after William Dargan, the contractor. The name was subsequently changed to 'Queen's Island', in honour of Queen Victoria. In 1853 a yard for iron shipbuilding was laid out on the Queen's Island and was leased by Robert Hickson, and later by Harland & Wolff. The Harbour Commissioners continued to encourage shipbuilding by providing additional shipyards on favourable terms, and by building bigger dry docks as the size of ships increased. All three Belfast shipyards expanded far beyond their original boundaries; Harland & Wolff had under 2 acres in 1859 and over 300 acres in the middle of the twentieth century, Workman Clark expanded from 4 acres in 1880 to over 100 acres, and Mac-

Ilwaine & Lewis began with 1 acre and had 17 acres when they gave up shipbuilding. The ability to expand was of great importance when the fashion in passenger ships, and later tankers, changed to mammoth size, and compelled the shipbuilders to lay out new yards to build them. Not only was land available, it was also eminently suitable for shipbuilding; it was flat, not much above sea level, and there was ample room for launching ships. This all helped to keep down the shipbuilders' costs. Outside Belfast no comparable shipbuilding sites existed in the north of Ireland, and only at Londonderry were there dry dock facilities. This was a further factor restricting shipbuilding, and consequently marine engineering, to Belfast.

Shipbuilding and Marine Engineering

From the end of the nineteenth century, shipbuilding and marine engineering were closely associated at Belfast, and elsewhere in the United Kingdom. The shipbuilders made engines mainly for their own ships, and fluctuations in the output of engines followed the same pattern as the output of ships. In 1967, for instance, Harland & Wolff had a record output of ships at Belfast with almost 200,000 gross tons, while the output of marine engines at 276,700 ihp was only slightly below the previous record set in 1946.

The Geddes Committee on the shipbuilding industry pointed out in 1966 that the close connection between marine engineering and shipbuilding could no longer be regarded as essential for the prosperity of either industry, and suggested that in present conditions it would be more logical to have not more than four specialist marine engine works in the United Kingdom, preferably independent of shipbuilding operations.[17] The widening gap between the two industries was also emphasised by the chairman of Harland & Wolff, Mr J. F. Mallabar, in his statement to shareholders in 1967, when he said that the true basis of the company was shipbuilding at the Queen's Island yard at Belfast. The other activities such as ship repairing, marine engine building, electrical engineering, general engineering, structural steel work, and industrial housing were of secondary importance to the main issue. In the 1950s and 1960s the popularity of some types of marine engines declined, while the output of other types increased: in the United Kingdom the output in terms of horse-power of Burmeister & Wain diesel engines, the type made by Harland & Wolff, increased substantially, but the number of engines constructed decreased. In 1965 the engine works of Harland & Wolff on the Clyde were closed, and while the engine works at Belfast continued to be fairly fully employed until 1967, the number of orders for engines then began to decline. Orders increased again in 1968 but at the end of the 1960s it was not clear what the future would be for marine engineering, once the most important branch of the engineering industry in the north of Ireland.

CHAPTER SEVEN

Vehicles

Road

MUCH attention was devoted to roadmaking in Ireland during the eighteenth century, and by 1800 the roads were for the most part quite good. The Scots cart was introduced into the north of Ireland at the beginning of the nineteenth century and replaced the Irish car on the larger farms and for the transport of linen, but more primitive forms of transport continued to be used in the uplands well into the present century. The relatively peaceful and prosperous state of the north led to a steady demand for carts, and there were cartmakers at work in Belfast and in most of the towns and villages. There was less coachbuilding in the north than in the south of Ireland, where Dublin was the main centre of the trade. By 1914, the coachmakers had begun to feel the effects of the introduction of the motor car, and the market for horse-drawn vehicles soon declined. Some firms turned to the building of bodies for motor cars, but the demand decreased when the motor manufacturers began to supply standard bodies at prices well below those which the coachbuilders could quote. The building of bodies for buses and commercial motor vehicles was undertaken by a few private firms and by the Ulster Transport Authority, and there proved to be a continuing demand for this type of work. The cartmakers were not so much affected by the introduction of the internal combustion engine, for when tractors replaced horses, trailers were required to transport farm produce, and there are still firms in most provincial towns, and in Belfast, making trailers for tractors and motor cars, as well as trucks and trolleys.

By the 1830s, steam-powered road vehicles had been developed to the stage where they were reasonably reliable, but in Britain they were driven off the roads by stagecoach and turnpike owners, and from 1865 to 1896 restrictive legislation was in force, so that the further development of self-propelled road vehicles took place on the Continent rather than in the United Kingdom. There is only one reported instance of a self-propelled road vehicle being made in the north of Ireland in the nineteenth century. The Rowan brothers of Doagh in county Antrim took five years to design and build a steam coach which they demonstrated in Belfast in January 1836; it seated eight passengers inside and twenty outside, and was driven by two engines each of 10 hp. The boiler was placed at the back and was made of a number of tubes 'so that no danger could result from bursting'. The coach travelled on the level at 15 mph, and could climb an incline of one-in-nine at 6 mph. It was hoped that the coach would be employed immediately on a busy road like that from Belfast to Lurgan, and that 'some persons of influence would come forward to help its very talented projectors' but nothing seems to have been done to put the vehicle to commercial use.[1] The condition of the roads was blamed for its failure, for it was too heavy for roads built to carry only cart traffic. Steam road vehicles were not subsequently made commercially in the north of Ireland.

In the 1880s and 1890s, the bicycle did much to transform leisure activities; it also helped to introduce into the north of Ireland light engineering techniques not previously common in the area. Some two dozen local firms built cycles, none of them on a large scale: little capital was needed to set up in business, and only two or three workers were employed in each workshop. Apart from occasional custom-built racing cycles, the trade died out in the 1920s, by which time cyclemaking in the United Kingdom had become concentrated in the hands of a few firms in Britain engaged in mass production.

The production of motor cars in the United Kingdom began effectively in 1896; by 1913 nearly 200 makes of car had been placed on the market, and of these 100 had already been discontinued.[2] In the north of Ireland, only one make of car was successfully produced, although there was considerable interest in the possibility of motor-car manufacture, and a number of individuals built their own motor cars or motor cycles. The Chambers brothers, Robert, Jack, and Charles, began to build their 'Chambers' car in 1904 at Cuba Street in Belfast. Robert had been with Vauxhall Motors in London in the early years of the century and was one of the chief designers of the early Vauxhall cars. The Chambers car had many features unusual at the time but now commonly adopted, such as detachable wheels. The engines made by the company were at first two-cylinder horizontal, and later four-cylinder vertical types, fitted with the Chambers patent silent gearbox, but in their latter years the company bought their engines from British makers. The highest output was perhaps achieved in 1911 when fifty cars were made. In 1913 the firm moved to University Street where they produced models with cabriolet, limousine, and landaulette bodies, as well as vans and ambulances. In the same year a few cars were exported to Australia and New Zealand but the firm relied mainly on the local market and looked for support to the 'keen buying Belfast men'[3] who later deserted them when cheaper cars became available from Britain and America. In 1927 Chambers cars went out of production.

Two other cars were designed in Belfast and prototype models were built, but neither was put into large-scale production. The four-cylinder 'Fergus' car was designed by J. B. Ferguson and J. A. McKee, and one model was made in Belfast about 1910.[4] It was taken to America by J. B. Ferguson who later settled there; the car was produced in America but without much success. In 1918 J. A. McKee produced the six-cylinder 'OD' or 'Owner-Drivers' car with many special features designed for ease in driving and maintenance. One model was built which travelled over 250,000 miles before going out of service about 1936; the original body was damaged during the wartime air raids on Belfast, but the car is otherwise intact and is in the Transport Museum at Belfast. In 1919 J. A. McKee acquired premises on the Antrim Road in Belfast where he hoped to manufacture the 'OD' car, but it would have taken a great deal of money to get it into production and as this was not available at the time, OD Cars Ltd concentrated on repair work.

The motor-car makers in the north of Ireland had been interested in the cheaper types of car which soon became popular, but the local demand was insufficient to enable them to undertake large-scale production, and by the 1920s they were faced with serious competition from British and American mass-produced cars. Belfast lacked a tradition of light, repetitive, precision engineering, and even without the post-war depression it is doubtful whether motor-car manufacture could have been successfully continued in the north of Ireland in the 1920s. The Belfast firms were in exactly the same position as the many small motor-car manufacturers in Britain who were forced out of business at this period because they were unable to secure the economies of large-scale operations or to finance the introduction of improved production techniques. By the 1950s a car assembly plant required an output of some 60,000 units a year to secure the full benefits of large-scale flow production,[5] and this made the establishment of a locally based motor-car industry in the north of Ireland even more difficult. There were less problems in making special-purpose vehicles, and Short Brothers & Harland, for instance, have produced straddle carriers, fork-lift trucks, and armoured patrol cars. In the 1960s, the manufacture of motor-car components was introduced into the area, and it may be that in the future a motor-car manufacturer from Britain or overseas may find it advantageous to set up an assembly plant for cars or commercial vehicles in the north of Ireland. The main source of employment in connection with road vehicles locally has been the repair trade, which in 1961 employed some 10,000 people, including those engaged in distribution and petrol sales. The repair of motor vehicles has replaced the blacksmithing trade as one of the principal employers of engineering workers, and as the section of the engineering industry most widely dispersed throughout the province.

Rail

In 1836, 6 miles of railway were open in Ireland; by 1900 the mileage had increased to over 3,000. The Ulster Railway from Belfast to Lisburn was opened in 1839, and later became part of the Great Northern Railway (Ireland), linking Belfast with Dublin and Londonderry. The line from Belfast to Ballymena was opened in 1848; the main line was extended to Londonderry, a line was built to Larne, and a number of branch lines were added; the system became the Belfast & Northern Counties Railway, and was later run by the Midland Railway and then by the LMS under their Northern Counties Committees. The third railway from Belfast to centres in county Down was opened between 1848 and 1865. In addition to these 5 ft 3 in broad-gauge lines a number of 3 ft narrow-gauge railways were built in the north of Ireland in the 1870s and 1880s.

There was only one independent firm of main-line locomotive builders in Ireland, Thomas Grendon & Co of Drogheda; from the 1840s to the 1860s this firm built some of the early locomotives for the Irish railways, and also undertook rebuilding and repairs. Victor Coates & Co of Belfast bought some of the 6 ft 2 in gauge locomotives from the Ulster Railway when the gauge was reduced to conform to the new 5 ft 3 in Irish standard, and these were rebuilt to the new gauge. Two of them were purchased by the Londonderry & Enniskillen Railway in 1852, but they proved unsatisfactory and were scrapped four years later.[6] This is not surprising, for by the middle of the nineteenth century the building of locomotives required greater skill than a firm of general engineers could muster. Even Grendon's engines were inefficient, and the Irish railways either bought their locomotives from British makers or built them in their own works. In Britain, the railway companies had been forced to build locomotives as the private makers were unable to meet the demand both at home and overseas; in Ireland the difficulty was the lack of private firms with suitable engineering experience. Altogether, about a third of the locomotives for Irish railways were built in Ireland.

Dublin was the main centre of locomotive and carriage building, and at one time had three works in operation. At Belfast six engines were rebuilt at the works of the Ulster Railway in the 1860s, and from 1872 to 1882 fifteen locomotives were built, although major components like boilers were usually obtained from outside makers.[7] New works for the Great Northern Railway of Ireland were erected at Dundalk in 1887 and heavy locomotive work was transferred there from the old Ulster Railway workshops at Belfast. In the early years of the twentieth century some engines were remodelled at the Belfast works of the County Down Railway, but the only locomotive built there was created from bits and pieces in 1881 or 1882.[8] At the York Road works of the Belfast & Northern Counties Railway five 4-4-0 broad-gauge compound locomotives were built between 1901 and 1905, and four 3 ft narrow-gauge 2-4-2 compound tank locomotives between 1908 and 1920. In 1933, the LMS Northern Counties Committee introduced a new class of 2-6-0 Mogul locomotives, the first four were built at Derby, but the remaining eleven were built at York Road between 1934 and 1942. The York Road works undertook drastic rebuilding operations and in many cases created what were really new engines although they were not recorded as such; other engines were assembled after having been produced elsewhere, mainly at Derby. Locomotive building in the north of Ireland was an intermittent affair and the railway workshops were engaged mainly on repairs and overhauls. With their low traffic densities the local railways did not provide anything like as great a demand for rolling stock as those in Britain, and from the 1920s increasing competition from road transport undermined their position even further.

This situation led to experiments in the use of diesel traction in the 1930s, with a view to securing operating economies, and as these proved successful more extensive use was made of diesel units after the second world war, until in the 1960s steam locomotives had been replaced for all normal operating duties. In 1933 the Gardner Edwards company of Belfast supplied for a railway in Colombia a 3 ft gauge railcar which was given a trial run on the Ballymena & Larne narrow-gauge line before being shipped to South America,[9] but the firm does not appear to have made many other railcars. At the York Road works in Belfast, and at the Duncrue Street workshops during the existence of the Ulster Transport Authority, a total of seventy-one diesel power cars were built up to the beginning of 1968, some of them designed for both passenger and freight traffic.

In the 1930s, Harland & Wolff built a number of diesel locomotives for the local railways, and for the Sudan and South America, as well as power units for other railways overseas. A diesel shunting engine supplied to the LMS in 1934 was one of the few engines built in Ireland for a railway in Britain. After the second world war, Harland & Wolff carried out heavy overhauls on ten Northern Counties steam locomotives, but they did not continue locomotive building or repair work.[10]

The major Irish railways undertook carriage and waggon building, but few local independent firms carried out carriage building for long. At Belfast in the 1860s, Thomas Firth made switches, crossings, couplings and other railway equipment at his works on the Falls Road, and he built carriages and waggons for some of the railways in the north of Ireland, including the Londonderry & Lough Swilly Railway. Firth had been engineer of the Belfast & Holywood Railway, and this no doubt explains his entry into the railway equipment business. At May Street in Belfast, R. Milligan made track inspectors' pedal trolleys; some of these were exported and there is one in the Transport Museum at Belfast. It was the demand for equipment for the local railways which led James Combe to establish the Falls Foundry in 1845, but in the long term the chief demand from the railways which was supplied by local firms was for iron castings. Some tramcars were built in Belfast up to the 1930s, and one of the three steam engines for the Cavehill & Whitewell Tramway was built by the Belfast firm of Wm Grant & Co in the 1880s, but the parts appear to have been supplied by Kitsons of Leeds.[11]

Tramcars have been replaced by buses, and in spite of the economies of using diesel instead of steam power, railway traffic has declined greatly; as a result of the closing of unremunerative lines, the railway network and the industries serving it in the north of Ireland, have been reduced to a fraction of their former extent.

Aircraft

During the first decade of the twentieth century there was great interest in flying and numerous foolhardy enthusiasts built aeroplanes and attempted to fly them, without appreciating the dangers to life and limb involved in the flying of untested machines by inexperienced pilots. In the north of Ireland the best-known aviator of the period was Harry Ferguson who became interested in aeroplanes after building and racing his own motor cycle and motor car. He first flew his 34 ft span monoplane at Hillsborough in county Down on 31 December 1909, but his record for the first flight in Ireland was not officially established until the following year. He continued flying up to 1912, but no great improvement was made in the design of his aircraft and control in flight was not good. There were numerous crashes and he himself suffered injuries, as did some of his passengers; his mechanic Joe Martin lost several teeth on one occasion.[12] Lilian Bland of Carnmoney near Belfast was probably the first woman to build and fly her own aeroplane. Her 27 ft 7 in span biplane, named *Mayfly* because of its unknown flying qualities, first flew under power at Randalstown in August 1910. Miss Bland described herself as an aeronautical engineer, and she advertised in *Flight* offering to build gliders and powered planes; since she had no capital left and no production facilities it is just as well that she received no orders. Her biplane was underpowered and it would have been beyond her financial resources to redesign it, so she wisely accepted her father's offer to buy her a motor car on condition that she gave up flying.[13] In 1916, Harland & Wolff began to produce DH6 and Avro training aircraft, and in 1918 in conjunction with Handley Page commenced manufacture of V/1500 four-engined 150 ft span bombers. These were capable of carrying 3–5 tons of bombs and were the largest aircraft designed at the time. However, the heavy bomber policy was adopted too late for the planes to play a significant role in the war, and only four of the twenty ordered had been completed when the contract was cancelled following the armistice.[14]

It was again the need to expand the production of military aircraft that led to the revival of the aircraft industry in the north of Ireland. In 1938 production began in a Government-built factory at Queen's Island managed by Short & Harland Ltd, formed by Harland & Wolff and Short Brothers of Rochester, who had been the first commercial makers of aircraft in the world, and had subsequently specialised in the manufacture of seaplanes and flying boats. Apart from the strategic consideration of distance from the Continent, the factory had the advantages of the Belfast harbour airport on the one side and a deep-water berth on the other where aircraft carriers could load and unload planes, as well as open water for flying boats. Production began with contracts for fifty Bristol Bombay transport planes, followed by 150 Handley Page Hereford bombers. In 1940 the works began to manufacture the four-engined Stirling, the first of the heavy bombers, which entered operational service with the RAF in February 1941. In the later stages of the war, modified Stirling aircraft were produced for use as glider tugs and paratroop transports, and played an important part in the invasion of Europe. Altogether 2,381 Stirlings were built in six years, more than half of them at Queen's Island and by the satellite factories and sub-contractors in the north of Ireland. The other military aircraft built at Belfast during the second world war was the Sunderland flying boat, of which 133 out of a total of 749 were constructed at Belfast between 1942 and 1946. This remarkable aircraft first flew in 1937,

Page 107   (above) *Short Stirling bomber;* (below) *Short Belfast freighter*

Page 108   (above) *Rolls-Royce Spey by-pass turbofan jet engine—parts made in Belfast* (below) *Short Seacat ship-to-air missiles*

and was not withdrawn by the RAF until 1959, after a record twenty-one years of operational service; it continued in use with the New Zealand air force until 1967.

In 1943 the British Government took over the management of the Short Brothers factories under the Defence Regulations and acquired the whole of the share capital. In 1947, Short Brothers Ltd and Short & Harland Ltd were merged to form a new company, Short Brothers & Harland Ltd, with headquarters in Belfast. In 1948 the Rochester works closed down and most of the staff transferred to Belfast. When in 1954 the Bristol Aeroplane Company acquired a shareholding, the Government held 70 per cent of the shares and 15 per cent were held by both Harland & Wolff and the Bristol Aeroplane Company. After the war, when flying boats went out of fashion, Shorts devoted much effort to the design of new types of aircraft, and a number of prototypes were built; perhaps the most spectacular was the SC 1 vertical take-off and landing research aircraft. This achieved transition from level to vertical flight and back again in 1960, but was not developed further on account of economy cuts and lack of interest by the armed services. A number of other projects suffered from rapid changes in defence policy which prevented the company being able to secure orders for large numbers of any type of aircraft. In the 1950s Shorts built English Electric Canberras and Bristol Britannias under contract, and embarked on a programme of diversification which led to the production of analogue computers, hydraulic systems, special-purpose vehicles, carpet sweepers, aircraft seating, and missiles. In the 1960s the company continued to make fuselage sections and wings for other aircraft companies, and pods for Rolls Royce aero engines, but they also developed two important freight aircraft.

The Belfast was the first long-range strategic freighter for the RAF; when it entered service in 1966 it was the largest aircraft to have been used by the RAF, and could carry loads exceeding 11,000 cu ft in bulk and up to 77,000 lb in weight. Only ten were ordered for the RAF and no orders for civil versions were obtained, although

G

design work was done on a two-deck type with a hinged nose for easy loading of cargo. Much more successful was the smaller Skyvan which first flew in 1963, specifically designed for developing areas of the world where the ability to carry bulky loads into primitive airfields was required. It could carry up to eighteen passengers or a load of 4,600 lb. Up to April 1968 sixty-five Skyvans had been ordered and Shorts hoped to be able to sell a total of 500; together with missile systems the aircraft promised to be the company's main source of income until the 1970s.[15]

By 1939, the labour force in aircraft production at Belfast had built up to 7,500, and during the war the numbers doubled. By 1951 the total had fallen to 6,000 and the numbers fluctuated with changes in the fortunes of Shorts; the company did not appear to benefit greatly from the Government's majority shareholding, as far as continuity of production is concerned. Towards the end of the 1960s a more stable position had been reached and there seemed to be reasonable prospects that a labour force of 6,000 to 7,000 would be maintained for some years. After the ending of wartime subcontracting Shorts employed practically all the aircraft production workers in the north of Ireland. From 1946 to 1948 Miles Aircraft had a subsidiary factory at Newtownards for their Messenger and Gemini light aircraft, and from the 1960s Rex McCandless Aviation produced autogyros at Crumlin, but the numbers employed were small. As in the early days, there still seems to be a place in the aircraft industry for small firms with worthwhile products. From the beginning the aircraft manufacturers in the north of Ireland did not make their own engines, and it was only in 1966 that Rolls Royce began to produce small parts for their aero engines at Dundonald near Belfast.

CHAPTER EIGHT

Other Machinery

OTHER industries require engineering workers to install their plant and machinery, and to maintain it in good working order; large numbers of engineering workers are therefore employed outside the engineering industry. In 1961 there were in the north of Ireland some 8,500 men in engineering occupations employed in industries other than engineering. Major repairs and the making of spare parts often require more equipment than factory maintenance departments have available, and some engineering firms specialise in the provision of a repair and jobbing service. Since all other industries are potential customers this is an important sector of the engineering industry. Many local firms began by doing repairs and jobbing work, and later specialised in the production of plant and machinery for particular industries when they found a demand sufficiently stable to justify the risk. When they began making machinery they did not necessarily give up repair work; the provincial ironfounders in particular gained most of their business through repairs, even though they also made machinery for local needs.

Agriculture

Most rural blacksmiths in the north of Ireland made agricultural implements at one time or another, and a few attempted more advanced work when the Scots iron swing plough and other improved equipment for cultivation were introduced about 1800. There were a dozen plough makers in the area in the second half of the nineteenth century; the chief centre of plough making was Belfast, where the leading firm was James Gray & Co of May Street, founded in 1840. By 1890 they had won many prizes for their ploughs, and claimed that there was not a farm of any consequence in Ireland where their ploughs were not to be found.[1] The making of ploughs, grubbers, cultivators, and harrows declined from the end of the nineteenth century through the decrease in tillage, combined with increasing competition from large-scale manufacturers in Britain and America, and from makers in the south of Ireland, especially at Wexford. When the demand for horse-drawn ploughs decreased only a few local firms undertook the production of ploughs and other implements for use with tractors.

The extensive cultivation of the potato in the north of Ireland led to a substantial demand for spades, and the cutting of peat for fuel required specially designed spades or 'slanes'. These were made in small mills where the metal was formed when hot under a water-powered tilt hammer. In spite of the fact that spade mills were often called 'founderies', they did not melt their metal and cast it in moulds; they were more frequently referred to as 'plating mills'. In the first half of the nineteenth century there were some thirty spade mills in Ulster, not all of them continuously at work; the industry declined rapidly after the potato famine and at the beginning of the twentieth century probably only half a dozen were still in operation. Not only had the small country spade mills to meet competition from imported spades: in the 1880s Wm Gregg Sons & Phenix established a spade mill at their Union Foundry in Belfast and began to produce annually some 20,000 dozen steel spades and shovels of Canadian, English, and Colonial patterns.[2] Although the Union Foundry closed in the early 1930s, some of the small spade mills were kept in business by the large variety of designs which farmers insisted on. Each small region had special spades for most purposes, which did not commend themselves to farmers in other areas; altogether some 250 types of spade were made in the north of Ireland. By the end of the 1960s only one spade mill in Northern Ireland was still in commercial operation, at Templepatrick in county Antrim, but there was another still making spades at the Ulster Folk Museum at Cultra in county Down. This mill had originally been established at Coalisland in county Tyrone, but had ceased production many years before it was dismantled and transferred to Cultra.

There were considerable differences between the provinces of Ireland in the use of agricultural machinery. Most of the mowers and reapers were used in the south, and by the end of the nineteenth century the only Irish makers were to be found in Wexford. In the first decade of the twentieth century more than two-thirds of the threshers in Ireland were in use in Ulster, and this concentration had resulted in the thresher being the main type of agricultural machine made in the province. Improved threshers were introduced from Scotland after 1800, and were made by most of the provincial ironfounders and by a few of the Belfast firms, the principal makers were perhaps H. Kennedy & Son of Coleraine. Many of the horse-operated threshing machines were designed so that the drive could be diverted to a winnowing machine in the same loft, or to a churn on the ground floor. Land-rollers were also made in large numbers in the north of Ireland, but while many potato diggers and potato

Threshing machine by H. Kennedy & Son Ltd, Coleraine

sprayers were used in the area, few of them appear to have been made locally. In recent times local firms have concentrated on the production of fairly simple farm equipment which is bulky in relation to its value, and on making meal mixers and grain driers.

In the 1850s the Musgrave brothers in Belfast began to produce their patent stable and cow-house fittings. They may have been encouraged to do so by the change from tillage to livestock farming in Ireland, or by the national enthusiasm for horses; by the end of the century they had built up an international reputation for their products and had exported them far afield. The fittings were expensive and were supplied mainly to royalty, the nobility, and the armed forces, rather than to farmers; it was claimed that the extensive use of cast iron made them practically indestructible and they did not harbour disease. Musgraves became ironfounders by appointment to the Empress Frederick of Germany, the Queen-Regent of Spain, the Prince of Wales, the Duke of Coburg, the King of the Netherlands, and the Khedive of Egypt, and they supplied stable fittings to many of the great engineers of the period such as Sir Joseph Whitworth, Monsieur Eiffel, Chevalier Whitehead, Lord Armstrong of Elswick-on-Tyne, and Herr Friedrich A. Krupp of Essen.[3] This was one of the few instances of agricultural equipment made in the north of Ireland becoming established in the world market. Although Harry Ferguson became interested in the use of tractors in agriculture when he was supervising their operation and maintenance during the first world war on behalf of the Department of Agriculture in Ireland, and in spite of the fact that much of the development work on his tractor and the revolutionary three-point linkage and hydraulic lift for implements was carried out in the north of Ireland, his ploughs and tractors were not manufactured in the area, but in America and Great Britain.[4]

The demand for agricultural implements in Ireland, especially in the south, was restrained by the fact that improvements and the provision of equipment were generally the responsibility of the tenant, who was seldom able or willing to invest in them, subject as he was to rack renting, and lacking security of tenure. The improvement in the position of the tenants did not take place until well after the middle of the nineteenth century, after the expansion of implement making in Britain and America. The potato famine and the decline in tillage in Ireland also reduced the local demand for implements at a time when competition from overseas was increasing. This led to the bulk of agricultural implements being imported. Even if the land system had not been unsatisfactory, the size of Irish farms in the nineteenth century would have discouraged the use of machinery. A steam plough and its equipment costing £1,200 to £1,600 might have been justified on a 600 or 800 acre farm in Norfolk or the Lothians, but would have been completely uneconomic on an Irish farm of 30–40 acres.[5] Even in Britain, steam ploughing and threshing were largely jobs for the contractor, as the capital expenditure was too great for the average farmer. No heavy agricultural machinery was made in Ireland; the small amount used was supplied from Britain and America. In more recent times the small size of farms restricted the rapid adoption of tractors, and, although the numbers have increased substantially since the second world war, the market is still too small to justify their production locally.

Food, Drink, Tobacco

Corn mills became common in the north of Ireland in the seventeenth century. They were mostly manor mills scattered throughout the countryside, and they secured their custom through the old feudal practice of requiring the tenants to have their corn ground at the landlord's mill. Until after the middle of the nineteenth century stones were still used for milling, and the output of each mill was small. The main structure was of wood or stone, and metal was used for part only of the gearing; although the mills were not very efficient, local engineering firms did not develop improved milling machinery. A great change in the flour-milling industry resulted from the replacement of millstones by iron rollers. This process was developed in Hungary about 1840 and was generally adopted in the larger mills in Ireland between the 1860s and 1880s; the gradual reduction of the wheat between a series of rollers produced better qualities and greater varieties of flour, and greatly increased the output.

As the new machinery was expensive and particularly suited to hard imported wheats, there was a rapid reduction in the number of mills in the north of Ireland and a concentration of the large mills at the ports. The number of mills had been declining already on account of the repeal of the corn laws and the after effects of the famine, but the introduction of roller milling coincided with heavy imports of cheap American flour, and this proved too much for many of the country mills. In the 1880s Victor Coates & Co of Belfast made roller mills and centrifugal flour-dressing machines, but after they closed in 1905 no local firm continued production there, although some parts of the equipment, including rollers, were made in Belfast.

A side effect of the potato famine was the rapid increase in the use of maize for human food and later for cattle feeding; in the 1880s J. H. Greenhill of Belfast developed his patented disintegrator which reduced maize to a fine meal without the use of millstones. Bakery machinery was also made in Belfast, but other branches of the food processing industry were not large enough to encourage the local production of the specialised machinery which they required.

Brewing was one of the first industries to be affected by the industrial revolution, but the change consisted in the adoption of large-scale operations rather than the extensive use of power-driven machinery. The metalwork required in breweries consisted mainly of copper vessels to contain the product at various stages in brewing. A large amount of copperwork was also required in distilleries, and a few firms in the north of Ireland specialised in this, but they turned their attention mainly to marine work when the brewing and distilling industries declined in the second half of the nineteenth century. The making of aerated waters has been an important industry in the north of Ireland from early in the nineteenth century, and usually there have been some thirty firms engaged in the trade. From the 1850s until the 1930s there was a regular export trade in aerated waters from Belfast; this was one of the few products for which the town had a good supply of raw material readily available, as pure and suitable water could be obtained by drilling deep wells down to water-bearing strata far beneath the surface.

Aerated water machinery was being made in Belfast early in the nineteenth century. In 1800 Job Rider, who was a clockmaker and later a partner in the Belfast Foundry, had invented a machine 'for impregnating water of different kinds with fixed air', and he believed the products would equal 'the waters imported from London, which had been found useful in the cure of complaints of the stomach and kidneys'. He was prepared to sell his 'single and double aerated alkaline waters' cheaper than they could be imported, but he was not offering to sell his machines.[6] In the second half of the nineteenth century there were five firms in Belfast and one in Newry making aerated water machinery, but by 1914 only one was still in business, and the making of these machines appears to have ceased in the 1920s. In 1898 the Turn-Over Filter Company in Belfast began the production of water filtration plants for industrial purposes, urban supplies, and for use on board ship. The company took its name from the filter patented by Balfour Bramwell, which could be turned over to allow the sand used as a filtration medium to be cleaned out periodically by a reverse flow of water. These and later types of filters were supplied to local water boards, some were installed in ships built in Belfast, and many were exported, especially to Africa. The company went out of business in 1959.

Although the Irish are inveterate tea drinkers, it could hardly have been foreseen that Belfast would become the principal producer of tea-estate machinery. In 1864 Samuel Davidson (later Sir Samuel) went from Belfast to India as an assistant on an Assam tea plantation; he soon acquired his own estate and introduced improvements in the then primitive methods of tea production. In 1869 and 1870 he took out patents for a tea-drying machine and a tea roller; in 1878 he had an improved drier made in Belfast and shipped for demonstration in India, from whence he returned with a large number of orders. Some of the first tea driers, like the demonstration model, were made by Ritchie Hart & Co, but in 1881 Davidson established his own works in Belfast and gradually developed a complete range of tea-estate machinery—withering machines, leaf rollers, driers, sorters, and packers, under the Sirocco trade mark. In the 1880s a Victory tea-drying machine was developed by an Ulsterman called Nelson, who had also been in India; some machines were made at the Falls Foundry in Belfast but the drier was not a success. Experiments with tea driers led Davidson to invent a centrifugal fan to provide better draught, and this resulted in the expansion of the firm's business into the field of ventilation. Machinery was also developed for coffee estates, and the production of tea machinery expanded until in the 1930s Davidson & Co supplied some 70 per cent of the world market for tea machinery.[7] After the second world war, tea machinery for India and Ceylon was made by a subsidiary company in India. While the Belfast works continued to make machinery for Africa and other countries where tea production was being developed, the output of tea machinery had been outstripped by other products and by the 1960s was only a small fraction of total output.

In the first half of the nineteenth century twist tobaccos were made on a small scale in many of the towns in the north of Ireland; in the 1840s there were some forty tobacco factories in the area. Tobacco had been grown in Ireland in the seventeenth century but its cultivation was suppressed by the Acts passed to encourage tobacco growing in Virginia, and the attempts to revive tobacco growing at the beginning of the twentieth century were not successful. The dependence on imported raw material resulted in the concentration of the industry in the ports, and the introduction of machinery drove out the smaller firms. Murray Sons & Co, one of the two large Belfast tobacco firms, was established in 1810 for the production of roll and twist tobaccos. In 1884 tobacco-spinning machines were patented by William Scott, then manager of Murrays; a number were sold to other tobacco manufacturers and some of these were made at the Falls Foundry in Belfast.[8] Thomas Gallaher started a one-man business in Londonderry in 1857 making twist tobaccos; in 1863 he moved to Belfast, and by 1891 had forty-five tobacco-spinning machines in operation.[9] In 1902, Gallahers began making cigarettes, and production expanded until the company had the largest tobacco factory in the world. In the first decade of the twentieth century there were three firms in Belfast making snuff and tobacco, two in Londonderry, and one in Newry. With increases in the scale of production, only Murrays and Gallahers were able to stay in business, but Gallahers opened a second factory near Ballymena and another factory was established by Carreras at Carrickfergus. A few of the Belfast engineering firms made tobacco-spinning machines, tobacco presses, or leaf strippers, but although spare parts were made locally, cigarette-making machines were not made in the north of Ireland until the Molins Machine Company established works at Londonderry in 1966.

Heating and Ventilating

The climate of the north of Ireland is not extreme, but it is sufficiently cold to create a demand for stoves for heating as well as for cooking. In the nineteenth century, some local firms made cast-iron stoves and cooking ranges, but the great majority of ordinary domestic stoves were imported from Britain. In the more specialised field of heating by convection and the use of heat to move air for ventilation Belfast firms were more successful in establishing themselves in the local and overseas markets. Samuel Davidson's interest in tea drying led to his development of stoves for heating by convection. These were designed to give out heat only in the form of hot air, while the parts which could be touched remained cool; this meant a greatly reduced fire risk, and little emission of dust. By the end of the 1880s, large numbers of Sirocco stoves were in use in local churches, halls, schools, workrooms, and linen-drying rooms.[10]

The Musgrave brothers had been making slow-combustion stoves in Belfast from 1855, and in the 1880s they introduced their Ulster convector stove. In 1891 production had reached about 100 per week, and Musgraves claimed that their Irish stove had become a household word on the Continent.[11] There must have been some truth in this, for by 1899 the firm had established a branch factory for stoves at Mannheim in Germany, and showrooms in Frankfurt and Paris. Although this type of stove went out of fashion for a time it was also useful for ventilating, as the heated air rose and drew in fresh air to replace it.

Ventilation was a problem in large passenger ships, and it was evident that the dust, heat, and moisture in linen mills was a cause of ill health, especially tuberculosis and bronchitis, amongst the operatives. Both in ships and mills fans were much more convenient for ventilating than stoves, but in the third quarter of the nineteenth century, when their use was becoming more widespread, most of the ideas, as well as the actual equipment for mechanical ventilation, came from abroad. In spite of the obvious local applications in shipbuilding and the linen industry, fan development in Belfast resulted from the solution to entirely different problems.

Samuel Davidson's early tea driers had relied on the draught induced by the furnace chimney to draw air through the trays of tea. However, even when the height of the chimney had been greatly increased there was still insufficient draught to draw the air through anything but a few lightly loaded trays. Positive pressure was needed, so he turned his attention to fans, and began a series of experiments which resulted in the development in 1898 of his highly efficient forward-bladed centrifugal fan. In conjunction with the drier this produced a large volume of hot air which reminded one of his friends of the hot wind that blows across the north African desert; the name Sirocco was later given to all the firm's products.[12] Fans, both centrifugal and axial flow types, were applied to many other purposes including forced and induced draught for boilers, the ventilation of mines, buildings, and ships, fume and dust removal, and air conditioning. The making of equipment for heating and ventilating eventually replaced the making of tea machinery as the firm's main activity.

In connection with a warm-air heating plant installed at the Empire Theatre in Dublin in 1900, Musgraves found it necessary to use a paddle-type fan to accelerate the flow of air in the ducts. This was such an improvement that the firm incorporated fans in later installations, and began to supply their Ulster fans for many other purposes.

The first world war led to an increased demand for fans; it was a rather ironic compliment to Davidson & Co that nearly every ship in the German fleet scuttled at Scapa Flow in 1919 was subsequently found to have been fitted with pre-war Sirocco fans. In the 1920s and 1930s the output of heating and ventilating equipment expanded; this was one of the few sections of the engineering industry in the north of Ireland which prospered during this period, and the export markets in Britain and overseas which had been established before the war were further developed. The second world war again led to a greatly increased demand for heating and ventilating equipment, and after the war a fairly steady demand continued. As heating and ventilating systems have to be designed specially for the circumstances in which they are to operate, and the necessary ducting is bulky and expensive to transport, local firms have advantages over competitors from Britain. A dozen mainly small firms supply much of the local market for air conditioning, heating and ventilating, and dust collection plant; this is one of the few fields in which local engineers have been able to set up in business successfully in recent years. On the other hand, to be able to export bulky equipment it is necessary to produce machinery which is technically superior to that made by competitors. Musgraves specialised in dust collection equipment and fans for power stations, as well as structural steelwork, and built up a substantial export business, but the company went into liquidation in 1965. Davidson & Co continued the development of equipment for cooling, drying, dust collecting, heating, ventilating, mechanical draught, pneumatic conveyance, and mechanical handling; for mine ventilation they produced some of the largest fans in existence, and they began to make large air preheaters for use in conjunction with their fans, mostly for power-station use. The company held its place as one of the principal engineering firms in the north of Ireland, and continued to export most of its output.

Armaments

In spite of the fact that the Falls Foundry made shells during the Crimean war and sharpened the sabres of the 6th (Inniskilling) Dragoons who fought at Balaclava, Belfast did not become a centre of the armaments industry in the nineteenth century; in this it was unlike the heavy engineering districts in Britain. During the first world war, in addition to increased output of ships, Harland & Wolff undertook the production of aeroplanes, and Davidsons made parts for submarines as well as large numbers of fans and heaters for war purposes. Most of the large engineering firms made shells, hand grenades, and parts for aeroplanes, and the Belfast Employers' War Munitions Committee organised the production of munitions by the smaller engineering works, by firms in the linen industry, and even in the workshops of the Belfast College of Technology. At the conclusion of the war armament production came to an end fairly rapidly.

One of the first changes brought about by the rearmament programme before the second world war was the establishment of Short & Harland's aircraft factory at Belfast. During the war, dispersal factories were set up, and subcontract work for Shorts was undertaken by local firms, principally Harland & Wolff and Mackies. Harland & Wolff again greatly increased the output of both naval and merchant vessels, and also produced tanks, setting up a tank assembly works at Carrickfergus. Landing craft were built at Belfast and Warrenpoint; factories were established at Antrim for the manufacture of torpedoes, at Laurelvale near Portadown and at Belfast for ball bearings, and at Bangor for incendiary bullet sleeves, and the repair of ships and aircraft employed large numbers of engineering workers. The existing engineering firms made shells, aircraft parts, gun components, and other forms of war material; as in the first world war the output of the small firms was co-ordinated by a local committee.

Mackies and the Falls Foundry made lathes for munition production, and Mackies organised fourteen dispersal units for making shells and aircraft parts, mostly in the premises of linen firms where the flax shortage had curtailed production. There was also a large demand for the normal products of many engineering firms, including electric motors and generators, and plants for heating and ventilating. At the end of the war munitions production declined, but Shorts developed missile systems and began to make armoured patrol cars, so that the north of Ireland retained its connection with the armaments industry. Perhaps the most important results of the increased wartime activity, apart from bringing Shorts to Belfast, were the expansion of the labour force including the introduction of women workers in large numbers for the first time, and the provision of additional factory space, which helped the post-war development of the engineering industry.

Other Industries

Up to the middle of the nineteenth century many small-scale industries existed in the north of Ireland to serve local needs, but increasing competition especially from Britain led to a gradual decrease in their numbers. Some industries such as soap-, starch-, and glue-making required little in the way of machinery; in other cases the demand for machinery was often insufficient to justify its production locally, and the engineering firms could only supply spare parts and undertake repairs. However, it is usually impossible to be certain that particular types of equipment were not made in the north of Ireland. The region had many inventive and enterprising engineers who were prepared to attempt to make machinery for practically any purpose; it did not follow, of course, that if they discovered how to make a particular type of machine that they could find a profitable market locally or sell it in Britain or overseas in the face of competition. For example, in 1832 the first of a new type of machine for making paper to be introduced into Ireland was made by Victor Coates & Co,[13] but the demand was insufficient for production to continue.

There was a fairly steady demand for general-purpose equipment such as pumps, valves, and air compressors, and these were made by a number of local firms. The making of plant for municipal gas works seems to have been largely in the hands of specialists from Britain, but small acetylene gas lighting plants suitable for private houses were made locally, and the making and repairing of gas meters has continued. With the exception of roller-fluting machines and roller-turning lathes for the flax-spinning industry, few machine tools were made in the north of Ireland once machine-tool production became a job for the specialist. In the 1880s the Falls Foundry appears to have made many special-purpose machine tools for use in the works,[14] and other local engineering firms may have done so too; by 1914, however, the design and performance of machine tools had advanced so far that it was better to buy them from expert makers. During the second world war, machine tools for munition production were made by Mackies and at the Falls Foundry, but since the war few metalworking machine tools have been made in the area, apart from lapping machines which give a highly accurate finish to metal components. The introduction of new production techniques has led to a demand by engineering

(above) *Horse-drawn plough by James Gray & Co of Belfast;* (below) *Spade-maker at work—Ulster Folk Museum*

Page 126   (above) *135 in diameter Sirocco two-stage axial flow mine fan;* (below) *128 in diameter Sirocco induced draught centrifugal power station fan on test*

firms for tools, jigs, and fixtures, and by the late 1960s some half-dozen firms were specialising in this type of work.

Services have to be performed where they are required, and this has protected service industries in the north of Ireland from overseas competition. Such industries did not necessarily have their machinery and equipment made locally, but local engineers had the opportunity to develop ideas in the course of installation and maintenance work. Laundry machinery, for instance, has been made at Larne, and by two or three firms in Belfast. Local engineering firms also had some advantages over competitors in supplying the construction industry in the north of Ireland with structural steelwork, metal windows, and elevators for passengers and goods. Transport costs made it difficult for firms in Britain to supply the local market for bulky but relatively inexpensive articles such as gates and railings, and sheet-metal products.

Local firms were also at an advantage in galvanising or electroplating, and in designing and supplying conveyors and mechanical handling equipment which had to be fitted into existing premises. The variety of plant and machinery required by other industries and the small local demand for any one type caused a number of medium-sized engineering firms in the north of Ireland to become machine makers; they would make machines for any industry, provided the customer supplied the drawings or a model to work from. Large engineering firms could afford to specialise and carry out their own development work; most small general engineering firms undertook repairs and the making of parts, but there was a place in the local market for a few firms which could provide an intermediate service.

This was undertaken by the more efficient among the provincial ironfounders; in Belfast perhaps the best examples were Ritchie Hart & Co who were able to produce the early models of Davidson's tea driers, Robert Craig & Sons, who in 1909 announced that they were prepared to make for the patentees any kind of machinery or engines,[15] and John Hind & Sons. Both Ritchie Hart and Craigs developed products of their own but continued to act as machine

H

makers; John Hind & Sons added machine making to their original business as specialists in the production of pistons and piston rings.

Since the second world war there has been a great change in the output of the engineering industry in the north of Ireland. Marine engineering, aircraft, textile machinery, heating and ventilating plant, and electric motors have held their position, but existing firms have developed new products, and many new engineering firms have been established in the area. The list of products continues to grow from year to year; up to the late 1960s perhaps the principal additions were data-processing equipment and computers, turbo-generators, telephone-exchange equipment, aero-engine parts, automobile components, tyre valves, rock-boring bits and other oilfield equipment, mechanical seals, scientific instruments, medical equipment, bulk storage containers, missile systems and special-purpose vehicles.

The making of cutlery and ball bearings has been reintroduced, and a new departure has been the production of domestic appliances such as carpet sweepers, vacuum cleaners, storage heaters, electric clocks, automatic tea makers, electric irons, and tape recorders, as well as gas or paraffin powered lamps, irons, and heaters. Some products introduced since the war have gone out of production, for instance cameras, record changers, radio receivers, and steel-mill equipment, but constant change is a feature of the engineering industry generally and not only in the north of Ireland. It has been clearly established, however, that new engineering firms can be set up successfully in the area; indeed by the late 1960s about half the labour force in engineering was employed by firms which commenced production in Northern Ireland since the war. In spite of the difficulties under which the industry operated, there is little evidence to show that there was in any field a substantial local demand for machinery which engineering firms in the north of Ireland did not attempt to meet; what is surprising is the extent to which machinery has been made for which there was no local market.

CHAPTER NINE

Pattern of Development

IN 1800, the engineering industry in the north of Ireland had just started to develop; during the nineteenth century it followed roughly the same pattern as in Britain, where textile machinery and steam engines for land or marine use were the principal products; armaments, however, were not made, little railway work was done, and the local demand was too small to encourage any firm to specialise in the production of machine tools.

In the late nineteenth and early twentieth centuries engineering firms in Britain began to make equipment used directly by the consumer, such as cycles, motor cars, and sewing machines, all of which were made only on a small scale in the north of Ireland. The local market for these, as well as for tools, implements, and hardware came to be supplied more and more from Britain and overseas. At the same time, an export trade developed in such equipment as tea-estate machinery, stable fittings, and heating and ventilating plant; textile machinery was supplied to the flax, hemp, and jute industries in other countries, and marine engines were made for ships built for owners who were almost all in Britain or abroad.

Between the two world wars, traditional markets were generally depressed, and the north of Ireland did not participate in the developments in light engineering during the period; only in a few fields such as the making of ventilating plant, jute machinery, and electric motors, did production and exports expand. The second world war, like the first, created a demand for munitions and other equipment; the post-war expansion led to a great diversification of the engineering industry, and the new products introduced were almost all intended for markets outside the north of Ireland.

The Local Market

As late as the eighteenth century, it has been argued, three-quarters of the Irish population lived by primitive forms of agriculture, and a cash economy extended little beyond the coastal fringe and the linen districts of Ulster; this maritime region was closely linked with Britain by ties of trade and credit,[1] and it was easy for British makers to supply the market for manufactured goods. For most of the nineteenth century, the poverty of the mass of the people meant that the demand for manufactured goods in Ireland was still low, and as conditions improved in the second half of the century the population declined, while competition from abroad increased. The Irish metal craftsmen had not supplied all the local demand for tools, implements, and hardware at the beginning of the nineteenth century, and their share of the market decreased as the century progressed.

The story of Irish manufacturing industries is one in which 'decline' and 'decay' occur with monotonous regularity; by the end of the nineteenth century most of them were concentrated in the north, but even there insufficient industry existed to provide a large local market for machinery and specialist engineering services. In spite of the advantages of being close at hand for local customers, engineering firms found it increasingly difficult to withstand competition from Britain and overseas.

The reasons for the poverty of the Irish market were mainly economic, but the situation was aggravated by political factors. The wars of the sixteenth and seventeenth centuries might not in themselves have had a permanent effect on Irish industry, but they were accompanied by scorched earth policies, by the destruction of most of the ironworks, and by massive land confiscations which left the seed for centuries of strife and bitterness and laid the foundations of a land system which did much to hinder economic progress in Ireland. It was unfortunate that the long period of unsettlement hindered technical development at a time when in Britain the stage was being set for the industrial revolution. During the eighteenth century, the mercantilist policies followed by the British Government sought to suppress any Irish industry likely to have an adverse effect on British interests, and to channel trade through British ports. The restrictions on trade had a depressing effect on Irish industry as a whole, but it is impossible to say how extensive the metal trades in Ireland might have become had Government policy been different. The worst result, as with the wars of the previous two centuries, was perhaps to restrain Irish industrial development when rapid progress was being made in Britain.

To offset the effects of restrictions on external trade, the Irish Government in the eighteenth century made grants for the development of industries and transport facilities, but with little positive result.

From 1710 to 1828, substantial sums were expended by the Government-sponsored Linen Board to encourage the linen industry, which did not constitute a threat to British prosperity. The Board endeavoured to introduce improved machinery for scutching, hackling, spinning, and thread making, through the granting of premiums and the supply of the latest types of equipment. Their efforts met with a poor response, and the making of flax machinery did not become established in Ireland until after the Linen Board had been dissolved. Government efforts to encourage the coal and iron industries were no more successful. In the last two decades of the eighteenth century, the Irish Government had greater legislative independence and attempted to encourage industry by bounties and protecting duties. One consequence was the expansion of the cotton industry, and the ensuing demand for steam engines and machinery led to the establishment of engineering works.

The failure of Government efforts to assist Irish industry in the eighteenth and early nineteenth centuries was due largely to jobbery and the lack of an efficient administrative machine. As Thomas Wallace put it in 1798, 'for many years the funds of the Irish treasury were lavished in futile and abortive projects, until the public mind became so disgusted with works carried on, or aided, by public grants, that at length no aid could be obtained for the most laudable and necessary undertakings'.[2] State action in Ireland in the nineteenth century was chiefly concerned with land tenure, and with relief schemes and public works which provided employment for unskilled workers but required little machinery. As the century progressed, it became obvious that no solution had been found to the problem of declining Irish industries; numerous commissions informed the Government of conditions in Ireland, but the climate of opinion was opposed to direct Government action, and suggestions for public enterprise, such as the nationalisation of the railways, were ignored.

In 1891 the Congested Districts Board was set up, with power to foster industries in the congested districts in the west of Ireland, but the Board confined its attention largely to tweed and lace making in the home, and did not undertake the ownership or management of any industrial undertaking. A Department of Agriculture & Technical Instruction for Ireland was set up in 1899, but it had power to promote only rural industries, and used this power to little effect. A committee of inquiry was appointed to consider the operation of the Department, and in 1907 W. L. Micks presented a minority report recommending the establishment of a development department spending annually some million pounds and exercising over the whole of Ireland powers similar to those of the Congested Districts Board.

This commended itself to the Government of the day no more than his other revolutionary proposal, that the Government should defray the cost of instructing employees in the early years of a new industry.[3] Industrial as well as political opinion was generally opposed to Government assistance for industry. Belfast, its spokesmen felt, had achieved its prosperity because its people were 'the most industrious of any in the United Kingdom', not because the Government had given financial support through the Linen Board, or because of any other outside assistance.[4]

The Union between Great Britain and Ireland took effect in 1801; though political in origin, it had important economic consequences, for it brought Ireland into close association with the most progressive industrial economy in the world at that time. Such protection as Irish industry enjoyed was removed by 1826, with disastrous results for many Irish firms, and the position was aggravated by the potato famine; in the second half of the nineteenth century the numbers employed in manufactures in Ireland declined more rapidly than the population.

The Union of Ireland with Britain was blamed for destroying Irish trade and manufactures, and for most of the difficulties which faced the country during the nineteenth century. Nationalists felt that almost unlimited industrial expansion might be stimulated in Ireland by protection. This ignored the limitations of the home market, and experience showed that the only industries capable both of absorbing a significant number of workers and affording a reasonable return were those which could compete in export markets.[5] Such industries were mostly in the north of Ireland, and it therefore suffered less from the economic effects of the Union than the southern provinces.

In the nineteenth century, while the Government did not concern itself directly with improving the local market for Irish manufactures, some sections of public opinion were mobilised in 'non-importation leagues', with the aim of encouraging the use of Irish rather than imported goods.

Organised movements for the support of home industry were nothing new in Ireland, and date back at least to Swift's essay in 1720 on *Proposals for the universal use of Irish manufactures*. Many of these movements were more anti-British than pro-Irish, and the thinking behind them was often confused. The interest aroused by the Great Exhibition of 1851 was reflected in Ireland by exhibitions held at Cork in 1852 and at Dublin in 1853; these encouraged a more positive approach to Irish industrial development, but little was done until the beginning of the twentieth century. The Glasgow

International Exhibition of 1901 aroused a new wave of enthusiasm which led to the establishment of a number of local industrial development associations in Ireland. As the engineering industry in Ireland at that period was making few goods for the consumer this movement had little effect on it. The energies of the industrial movement were devoted mainly to art and cottage industries, rather than to those which, though promising greater employment, would have required heavy capital investment.

Since the local market was so limited, it was almost inevitable that it should come to be supplied from Britain and other advanced industrial countries, even if Irishmen had consistently supported home industry. It is doubtful whether any degree of protection short of virtual prohibition of imports would have enabled Irish producers to supply all the manufactured goods required in Ireland. The decline of Irish manufacturing industries in the face of increasing competition was not just the result of inefficiency or lack of capital and technical knowledge, as was often claimed at the time. Even though tools and hardware were necessities, and the demand not subject to caprice and change of fashion, as early as 1796 English makers were supplying much of the Irish market, less on the grounds of better quality than because their goods were far cheaper.[6] The chief advantage the English manufacturers had was that production was on a much larger scale than in Ireland, and as the nineteenth century progressed the advantages of large-scale production became more and more important. Irish industries supplying only the home market were seldom able to reach the optimum size which would have minimised costs of production.

Improvements in transport forced the rural smiths and other small working capitalists to compete with large-scale specialists. In Britain they had to attempt to produce on a comparable scale, or seek employment for wages in the large works; in Ireland there was usually no opportunity to operate on the same scale, and no wage labour available as an alternative. On the commercial side, too, the large-scale producer had advantages over the average Irish firm supplying the home market. Goods for direct use by the consumer, if they are to be distributed over a wide area, have to be produced before they are sold; credit facilities and a well-organised market are very important. In the nineteenth century these factors told in favour of large British and foreign firms supplying the Irish market in competition with local producers.

The small local market and the increasing pressure of competition adversely affected Irish producers of hardware and metal castings, and led to the decline of industries for which machinery might have been made in Ireland. The lack of employment discouraged the making of labour-saving devices, and when these began to be used in the second half of the nineteenth century, they were mostly imported. Engineering firms in the north of Ireland operating at less than the optimum size partially offset this disadvantage by concentrating on sectors of the market sheltered from overseas competition. This explains why so large a section of the industry provided a repair and jobbing service, and why the ironfounders did not mass-produce light castings. The textile machinery makers confined their production to preparing and spinning machinery for linen, hemp, and jute, where competition was limited; they did not make power looms, or textile printing machinery. Agricultural machinery, such as threshing machines, had usually to be installed in farm buildings, and heating and ventilating plant had to be erected where it was required, and this favoured the local maker. In the first half of the nineteenth century local makers of steam engines were protected in some degree by transport difficulties; towards the end of the century smaller power sources such as internal combustion engines and electric motors were developed, and these could readily be imported. The north of Ireland was more prosperous than the southern provinces, but even in the north the local market was not large enough to encourage many firms to produce metal goods for the consumer. The concentration of Irish manufacturing industries in the north made the region the chief centre of the engineering industry in Ireland by the beginning of the twentieth century; if the industry was limited in extent this was due to the smallness of the market, and not to any inability or unwillingness on the part of local engineering firms to produce equipment for which there was a demand.

There has been little change in the position since the beginning of the century. The first world war did not create any continuing addition to the local demand; in the 1920s and 1930s engineering firms in the north of Ireland were cut off from any markets they may have had in the south, and the local market suffered from the depressions in shipbuilding and the linen industry. The development of new types of light engineering, especially in the south of England, gave competitors additional advantages. During and after the second world war, new industries were introduced which improved the local market for goods and services provided by engineering firms; the local economy became much more prosperous than before the war, but the scale of production had again increased and most of the local market for plant and machinery, as well as consumer goods, continued to be supplied by firms outside the north of Ireland.

Overseas Markets

In Britain, most branches of the engineering industry were established to fill some local need, and then often expanded to a scale beyond the capacity of the home market; manufacturers generally did not attempt to supply a foreign market before winning business nearer home. In Ireland, however, the position appeared to be different, at least from the latter part of the nineteenth century. C. H. Oldham warned in 1908 that anyone might 'set up an industry in Ireland if he saw a market for his production in England, Scotland, or at the ends of the earth, but he would make a mistake and lose his money if he was aiming at a market in Ireland'.[7] This, no doubt, was an overstatement, but by that time many Irish industries did depend mainly on export markets, and in many sectors it had become impossible to set up new enterprises unless a substantial proportion of the products could be exported.

This had not always been the case, however, for up to the middle of the nineteenth century the local market was protected by the difficulties in transporting heavy machinery. Before the American Revolution there had been a small export trade in cast-iron goods and nails from Ireland to the American colonies and to Britain, but the independent metal craftsmen and engineering firms in Ireland concentrated on supplying the local market, and exports of machinery did not begin to build up until the late 1840s, when textile machinery began to be sent to Britain and to countries as far away as Egypt. There is no evidence to indicate that the British restrictions on the export of tools and machinery, which were in force up to the end of the first quarter of the nineteenth century, prevented any worthwhile export of machinery from Ireland.

Too much importance should not be attached to such early exports as the steam pumping engines sent to Egypt by MacAdam Brothers of Belfast about 1846. The Egyptians had obtained flax-scutching machinery from Belfast, and this may explain why they came to Belfast looking for steam engines; there is, however, no reason to suppose that they could not have obtained pumping engines as good, if not better, elsewhere in the United Kingdom. MacAdam Brothers did not follow up their ventures into the export market, and in general few of the engineering firms established in the north of Ireland before 1850 became regular exporters of machinery. This was in spite of the fact that Britain was still the workshop of the world and there were few difficulties in selling machinery abroad.

It was not until the last quarter of the nineteenth century that local engineering firms began to build up an export trade in equipment other than textile machinery, and marine engines began to be made in large numbers for ships built in Belfast for owners in Britain and overseas. The development of export markets was facilitated by Britain's free trade policy, by the expansion of the Empire, and by the emergence of a world economy as communications improved.

The increase in engineering exports, however, took place when the United Kingdom had lost its near monopoly in the making of machinery, during and after the 'great depression' of the 1870s and 1880s, when profit margins were falling and overseas competition increasing. The comparatively new firms beginning to export from the north of Ireland must, therefore, have been able to produce at costs competitive with other engineering centres; one factor in their favour was that they were not burdened by obsolete equipment, or over-development of fixed resources. Tariff restrictions introduced towards the end of the nineteenth century by countries wishing to expand their own manufactures did not adversely affect the exports of capital equipment, for this was still needed by developing countries.

Between the wars, exporting industries were hampered by the depression of traditional markets, additional tariff barriers, unstable currencies abroad, and the over-valuation of sterling on the return to the gold standard. The powers given to the new Northern Ireland Government under the Government of Ireland Act of 1920 did not permit it to interfere with external trade, or to alter rates of exchange, and it was unable to give special assistance to firms in the export trade. In spite of the difficulties, some local engineering firms such as Davidsons and Mackies were able to increase exports, but the period was generally one of stagnation.

After the second world war, the firms which were already established in the British or foreign markets were able to maintain their position, for in spite of increasing competition, engineering has benefited from the expansion of industry in developing countries and the movement to reduce barriers to trade between developed countries. As in the past, local firms which wished to enter the export market have sought to benefit from specialisation rather than mass-production. Concentrating on a restricted group of customers, with the aid of specialist knowledge or patents, they have been able to build up goodwill and keep in close touch with the needs of customers, so that the effects of competition have been minimised.

The making of specially designed equipment has advantages also on the commercial side; it has generally to be sold before it is produced, and there is therefore less need for an organised market and extended credit facilities than with mass-produced goods.

Since the second world war, the position has been complicated by the fact that many of the new engineering firms established in the north of Ireland have been production units only with no responsibility for establishing and maintaining markets, this being the function of the parent company in Britain, Europe, or America. While this arrangement has some drawbacks, it has the advantage that the local engineering industry has been able to benefit from the experience and organisation of established firms in greatly increasing its exports to Britain and overseas.

Imports and Exports

It is difficult to get a clear picture of the imports and exports of plant and machinery in the north of Ireland. Up to the beginning of the twentieth century no accurate figures existed, and after 1935 the value of ships and aircraft was included with miscellaneous manufactured articles to avoid disclosing the exports of individual firms. There appears to have been at all times a large net import of metals, tools, and hardware, but this is what would be expected in a small region with no useful resources of coal or iron; the only significant metal export was of iron scrap. Imports of vehicles consistently exceeded exports, and this was also the case with machinery during the nineteenth century. From 1860, exports of machinery increased more rapidly than imports, and in 1906 the value of exports exceeded that of imports; until 1934 exports and imports were roughly equal in value, and after that date, as far as can be ascertained, exports were generally more valuable than imports.

Ships and their machinery formed the largest engineering export group, followed by textile machinery. For the years when figures are available it appears that the exports and imports of textile machinery were roughly equal in value. This is quite likely, for while machinery was exported for preparing and spinning flax, hemp, jute, and other fibres, power looms and other types of textile machinery had to be imported. By the 1960s engineering had become the principal exporting industry in the north of Ireland, sending its products mainly to Britain, Europe, India and Pakistan, Central and South America, Africa, Australasia, and the Far East.

In 1965, the goods sold by firms employing twenty-five or more persons to customers outside the United Kingdom were valued at more than £21,000,000; to customers in Great Britain at nearly £49,000,000, and to customers in Northern Ireland at less than £9,000,000. In addition some £7,000,000 was charged for work done to firms outside Northern Ireland, and £9,000,000 to firms in Northern Ireland.[8] This emphasis on production for export while the local market was supplied largely from outside the area was not peculiar to the engineering industry in the north of Ireland; it was characteristic of the Irish economy both north and south from the nineteenth century.

The Scale of Production

By the middle of the nineteenth century there were some twenty engineering firms in Belfast employing nearly 2,400 workers. The three firms making steam engines each employed 250 men or more; four of the six textile machinery makers had at least 100 employees; most of the other firms employed less than fifty people.[9] In 1851, fewer than one in nine of the engine and machine makers in Britain employed forty or more men, while seven of the nine such firms in Belfast had over 100 workers; in Britain there were only twenty-five engineering firms employing more than 200 people, but there were five firms in Belfast each employing 250 or more,[10] and by the late 1860s both Harland & Wolff and the Falls Foundry had over 1,000 workers. There was already a marked difference in the scale of certain metal working operations; in 1870 the average number employed by British firms engaged in metal manufacture was thirty-four, in iron shipbuilding 570, in making machinery eighty-five, but in producing nails and rivets only eight.[11]

As has already been noted, market conditions in the north of Ireland after the middle of the nineteenth century favoured either firms near optimum size selling part of their output outside the area, or small firms catering for some sheltered section of the local market. The gap steadily widened between the numbers employed by the large exporting firms and the small firms restricted to the local market, and the large engineering firms in the north of Ireland tended to be larger than their British competitors, while the small firms were smaller than similar establishments in Britain. This tendency continued until the 1930s, and in 1935 the numbers employed in mechanical engineering works in Northern Ireland were more than 70 per cent greater than the average for the United Kingdom, but in Northern Ireland foundries the numbers employed were only a quarter of the United Kingdom average.[12]

After the war, the situation changed with the setting up of new engineering firms, many of which, being branch establishments, were less influenced by the factors which determined the size of local firms, and the average size of firms in Northern Ireland was reduced below the level for the United Kingdom. In 1963, of the 347 engineering firms covered by the Census of Production of Northern Ireland, 243 employed less than twenty-five workers, but these firms accounted for only 4 per cent of the labour force. At the other extreme, 58 per cent of the labour force was employed by six large firms with over 1,500 workers each. The number of very small firms was decreasing, and the number of medium-sized firms increasing, but as in Britain the industry was still dominated by a comparatively small number of large firms.

Up to 1851, the engineering and shipbuilding industries in the north of Ireland had not begun to expand, and there was as yet no tendency for them to concentrate in Belfast or in Ulster. By 1911 there were 8,000 shipbuilding workers in Ireland, 7,000 of them in

Belfast, and 15,000 men engaged in making machinery and implements, half of them in Belfast. While the numbers engaged in engineering and shipbuilding in Belfast increased from 1,400 to 19,300
between 1841 and 1911, and more than doubled in Ulster over the
same period; taking Ireland as a whole, the increase was much less
marked. The decrease in the numbers of blacksmiths, nailmakers,
and other metal craftsmen in the whole of the country counter-
balanced much of the increase of employment in Belfast, so that the
total employed in engineering and shipbuilding in Ireland increased
only from 41,900 to 46,600 between 1841 and 1911.

In 1911, engineering and shipbuilding employed more men in
Belfast than the building and textile industries combined, and in the
rest of Ulster came second only to textiles. In the linen industry at
that period three-quarters of the labour force were women and the
total employed in textiles was therefore greater than in engineering
and shipbuilding; it was not until 1959 that the average numbers
employed in engineering and shipbuilding in Northern Ireland exceeded those in textiles. By 1926, engineering and shipbuilding had
become the main employers of male labour in manufacturing industries in Northern Ireland, not only in Belfast. In the early 1960s
engineering and shipbuilding were the largest employing group in
the manufacturing industries in Northern Ireland, and in 1965 employed 30 per cent of the labour force in manufacturing, a total of
some 54,000 people. While this was a significant proportion of the
total labour force in Northern Ireland, and some 70 per cent greater
than the total employed in similar industries in the Republic of
Ireland, it was only 2 per cent of the total engaged in engineering
and shipbuilding in Britain.

The industry in Northern Ireland was long dominated by shipbuilding and marine engineering, both in employment and output,
but by 1963 shipbuilding, marine engineering, and aircraft manufacture together had a net output slightly lower than the other
mechanical engineering firms in the area, with the output for electrical engineering accounting for the remaining 23 per cent of net

(above) *Data preparation equipment made by ICL at Castlereagh, Belfast* (below)
Sirocco two-stage drier for tea and other crops

Page 144   (above) *Goblin Teasmade by BVC Ltd, Castlereagh, Belfast;* (below) *Tape recorder Grundig Works (NI) Ltd, Dunmurry*

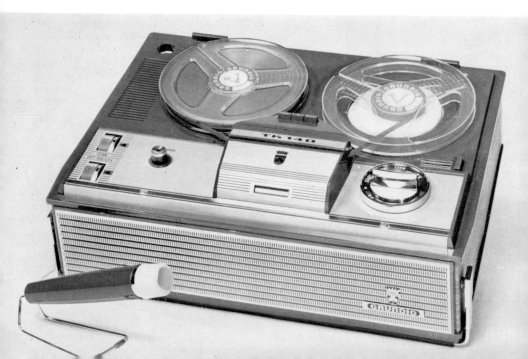

output for the industry.[13] This was a much better balance within the industry than in the past; there was still, however, little inter-dependence with other industries in the province. This has resulted from the fact that practically all raw materials have to be imported, and few of the products are used in other local industries.

Transport of Finished Goods

At the beginning of the nineteenth century the road system in the north of Ireland was good by contemporary standards; carts were used for carrying merchandise, and while they could not take loads much over a ton, the rates charged were low.[14] Canals had also been built to link Lough Neagh and the Tyrone coal district with Belfast and Newry. It was the lack of markets in the interior of the country rather than inadequate transport facilities which discouraged the expansion of engineering and the metal trades.

The building of the railways made it easier to transport heavy goods like coal, iron, and machinery, but the railways were built following roughly the lines of existing main roads which continued to compete for the limited traffic available, and eventually this was greatly to the disadvantage of the railways. There were in the north of Ireland too many lines of railway rather than too few; the hopes that the widespread building of railways would solve the problems of poverty and unemployment were not fulfilled. The railways provided some demand for iron castings, but did almost all of their own engineering work, and imported most of the locomotives used locally. Through carrying coal and raw materials, the railways encouraged the growth of industry in the provincial towns and so helped to increase the demand for machinery, but, in spite of their railways, many towns remained commercial rather than industrial centres. The railways also helped the provincial ironfounders to transport their products to their customers; the large exporting firms in Belfast, however, made little use of rail transport.

In the nineteenth century the Irish railways were continually

I

being criticised for inefficiency and for charging high and incon-
sistent rates; the most serious criticism was that their methods of
charging favoured overseas suppliers of the Irish market. Something
might have been done to improve the efficiency of the railways, and
the system of charges might have been better designed to encourage
local industry, but the basic trouble was that Ireland had not enough
internal traffic to provide a profitable freight business except on
some of the major lines, and therefore there was no hope of increasing traffic substantially by reducing charges.

After the 1920s, increasing competition from the roads worsened
the position of the railways; after the second world war, the mileage
of track was drastically reduced, and by the 1960s the railways
carried little freight for engineering firms in the north of Ireland.

The revolution in external transport by sea caused by the development of the steamship was more important for the local engineering industry than the building of the railways. Up to the middle
of the nineteenth century difficulties in sea transport had helped to
shelter Irish industries from British competition; the ships of the
period were small and the carriage of heavy equipment such as
steam engines was costly; it was therefore cheaper to import pig
iron and fuel and to make heavy iron castings in Ireland. There were
also considerable delays, especially in sailing from England to Ireland, as the prevailing winds were westerly. Before the days of
steam, according to Mr and Mrs S. C. Hall, a voyage to Ireland was
a 'kind of purgatory to be undertaken only in cases of absolute
necessity'; the journey usually took two to three days but often as
many weeks if the winds were unfavourable.[15]

A regular steamship service was established between Belfast and
Glasgow and Liverpool in the 1820s, and by the middle of the
century steamships operated between Belfast and a dozen British
ports. A service between Stranraer in Scotland and Larne was
opened in 1862 and was regularly maintained from 1872; steamship
services were also established linking other ports in the north of
Ireland with Britain. The low cost of transport by steamship altered

the commercial relations of different parts of Ireland; in the north it became cheaper to trade with Glasgow or Liverpool by sea than with Dublin by rail. Belfast developed closer commercial associations with the regions of heavy industry in Scotland and the north of England than with the south and west of Ireland. It seemed obvious to contemporary commentators that the improvements in sea transport would make it easier for producers in Ireland to sell on the British market, and many of the proposals for the development of Irish industry put forward in the second half of the nineteenth century, therefore, included suggestions for further improving sea communications with Britain. In his concluding address to the Social Science Congress in Belfast in 1867, John Mulholland claimed that 'no stimulus appeared so effective, simple or cheap for rousing the dormant energies of Ireland than a cheap and ready access to English demand for every branch of Irish production',[16] and in 1908 C. H. Oldham felt that Ireland's needs would be served better by improving transport than by applying protectionist policies.[17] Improvements in sea transport, however, facilitated trade in both directions and helped to supply the Irish market with cheap British manufactures, thus killing many small industries serving the local market instead of rousing the dormant industrial energies of Irishmen.

It became almost impossible for small firms in Ireland to compete in the production of light iron castings and of consumer goods made of metal. Engineering firms, except where they could depend on a local market sheltered from competition, had to develop products which could compete with those made in Britain or abroad. Since they also had to import their raw materials and fuel, this meant an avoidance of cheap, heavy articles, and a concentration on those which were valuable in relation to their weight and volume. In supplying the British market, firms in the north of Ireland were at a disadvantage in having to meet indirect transport costs for extra packing, damage in transhipment, and loss due to delays; to some extent these have been overcome in recent years by the use of containers or air freight.

In overseas markets, competitors usually had to meet similar transport costs, and the difference between starting from Belfast or a port in Britain was of little importance in a journey to the other side of the world. By the middle of the nineteenth century Belfast had an extensive trade with America, the Baltic, the Mediterranean, and the East; later, as steamships grew in size and the load required for economic operation increased, there were fewer direct sailings from Belfast, but it was still possible to secure reasonable rates if large enough cargoes were available. Like the railways, the shipping lines were criticised for inefficiency and for charging excessive rates, but again the main difficulty appears to have been the limited traffic available. Some sections of the engineering industry were fortunate, however, in having few problems in transporting their finished products; most of the marine engines made at Belfast were installed in ships built locally, and aircraft were able to fly out from the Belfast harbour airport or be hoisted aboard aircraft carriers at the wharf close to the factory.

The effect of transport costs on finished goods cannot have been critical, for otherwise it would have been impossible to supply from the north of Ireland textile machinery, fans, and tea-estate machinery to every available market in the world; freight costs did not hinder firms in Britain from competing in the Irish market.

Little reliable information was published on transport costs until recent years; the Census of Production for Northern Ireland in 1963 indicated that for engineering and shipbuilding transport costs amounted to 1·4 per cent of total sales. Within the industry the proportion varied from 1·1 per cent for the group which included marine engineering and aircraft construction, to 5 per cent for hardware, hollow-ware, and metal containers; perhaps as a result this latter group produced only 2·1 per cent of the net output for the industry. Transport costs in engineering were lower than the average for manufacturing industries, and very much lower than for some sections producing goods of low value in relation to weight. Since transport costs for raw materials were included in the total, the cost of transporting finished goods in the engineering industry probably amounted to less than 1 per cent of total sales.

The figures are based on total transport costs, not just the additional costs of operating in the north of Ireland; firms elsewhere have to transport raw materials and finished goods, but it would be difficult to draw any reliable conclusion as to the precise effect on the engineering industry in the north of Ireland of additional costs local firms may have to meet to deliver goods to customers. Transport costs have often been assumed to be higher than in fact they are, and have been blamed for difficulties inherent in the economic situation. In the absence of good local markets and cheap raw materials there were bound to be difficulties to be faced by all the industries in the area, including engineering; patterns of production had to be adapted to minimise these difficulties, of which transport was not the major one. The incidence of transport costs did, however, help to determine the products which could profitably be made in the area, and the most suitable locations for engineering firms.

Location of Industry

At the beginning of the nineteenth century, Dublin was the commercial capital of Ireland, Cork was the second city, and Belfast, Newry, and Londonderry were smaller towns than Limerick or Waterford. It was natural for the self-employed craftsmen to gravitate to the established commercial centres, and for new enterprises such as ironfoundries to be located there too. The Irish cotton industry became concentrated in the north, but in the early stages there were a number of mills in and near Dublin, and this led to the making of cotton machinery in Dublin in the 1780s. There were few attempts to make cotton machinery in the north of Ireland, where the making of flax machinery was not successfully established until the 1830s, after the adoption of power spinning for fine linen. The early use of steam engines in brewing, distilling, and cotton spinning in the south probably explains why steam engines were made in Dublin before they were made in the north.

In the first half of the nineteenth century, Cork was a more important marine engineering and shipbuilding centre than Belfast, and the shipbuilding industry in Belfast did not begin to expand until the 1860s. It was not until the second half of the century that Belfast emerged as the principal centre of the engineering industry in Ireland.

The industrial revolution was partly a revolution in transport; the building of the railways and the development of steamships enabled goods to be produced near their markets rather than at the source of raw materials. In Britain, shipbuilding tended to concentrate at the principal ports, and the making of textile machinery in the textile-producing districts; this was not just a matter of shorter transport but of personal contact and exchange of technical information, beneficial both to producers and customers. The need to be near the centre of the linen industry helped to expand the making of textile machinery in Belfast during the cotton famine, when linen was booming; afterwards the close association between the spinners and the machine makers was of great commercial benefit to both. Marine engineering was perhaps a special case, as it was undertaken mainly by firms already engaged in shipbuilding at Belfast.

Local demand was also responsible for the making of steam engines and electric motors, heating and ventilating plant, and some types of agricultural equipment, as well as repair and jobbing services. Market influences, however, cannot account for the production of tea-estate machinery in Belfast; this was perhaps partly the result of Sir Samuel Davidson's enterprise and partly due to the existence of skilled engineering workers in Belfast, who were able to make the equipment he had designed. Since most of the products made in Belfast were exported, their manufacturers cannot have been attracted mainly by the local market; they may have been influenced by the availability of labour or specialist services, and in recent times by Government financial assistance and advance factories with space for expansion, or by the unpredictable effects of individual enterprise. In the provincial towns the firms established in the nineteenth century were attracted by the local market for machinery and repair work, but few additional engineering firms were set up until extensive Government assistance became available after the second world war.

The engineering industry concentrated in Belfast originally because the town had become the main centre of Irish industry and therefore the principal market for machinery. The good port facilities which were provided reduced the cost of importing raw materials and coal, and of exporting finished goods. Once Belfast was well established in engineering, it became the natural focus for any new engineering activities in the area, and the concentration continued partly through the increase in the industry in Belfast and partly through its decline in the rest of the north of Ireland. This process continued until the late 1930s, and in 1935 over 90 per cent of the labour force was employed in Belfast.

After the second world war, the Government of Northern Ireland, largely through assistance to new industry, has helped to disperse a substantial section of the industry to the outskirts of Belfast and to the provincial towns. By 1963, 70 per cent of the labour force was employed in Belfast (including the large Castlereagh industrial estate), 12 per cent in Antrim and Londonderry, and 3 per cent in Down and Armagh, and the dispersal was continuing. The reversal of the tendency for the industry to concentrate in Belfast was helped by the changeover from the use of coal to electricity for power, for the cost of electricity does not vary with distance from the generating station. In the past the need to obtain coal as cheaply as possible had restricted engineering firms to the railway centres in the provinces or to sites in Belfast within easy reach of the docks.

Government Assistance

When the Government of Northern Ireland was set up, the cli-

mate of economic opinion was no longer entirely opposed to Government assistance for industry, but the Government of Ireland Act of
1920 withheld from the newly formed Government the power to
follow a policy of economic independence from Great Britain. Quite
apart from political considerations, Northern Ireland continued to
be united with Great Britain by close economic links, and an independent policy could not have been very effective. However, the
Northern Ireland Government was able to offer aids to industry
which were much more flexible than those provided in Britain;
generally a wider range of benefits has been available in Northern
Ireland and they have been set at a higher level than in Britain.

From the early 1920s, the Government undertook to guarantee
the payment of principal and interest on loans for carrying out
capital undertakings likely to promote employment. In the 1920s
and 1930s the projects assisted included shipbuilding, housing, the
purchase of machinery for industrial development, and the provision
of electrical generating plant; the shipbuilding industry in Northern
Ireland continued to enjoy this form of assistance after it had been
withdrawn in Britain.

Since the second world war, loans have been made or guaranteed
by the Government for industrial development or the reconstruction
of industries; important assistance has been given in particular to
shipbuilding and the aircraft industry. The derating of industrial
property to the extent of 75 per cent applied throughout the United
Kingdom from 1929 to 1959; in Britain it was reduced in 1959 and
abolished in 1963, but no such change was made in Northern Ireland. Another form of general assistance to industry, aimed at reducing recurrent expenditure, was the fuel rebate paid to manufacturing industries; this has helped to offset the additional cost of
importing fuel, and was again a form of assistance not available in
Britain.

Grants have been paid since 1932 to encourage the expansion of
existing industries and the setting up of new ones, including contributions towards the cost of plant, machinery, and buildings.

Grants have also been paid for the transfer of key workers and machinery, the training of labour, the employment of industrial consultants and management training. Government-built factories erected in advance of demand have been influential in attracting firms to locations outside Belfast, and special assistance has been given to projects offering unusual employment opportunities or to be located in areas of high unemployment. The activities of the Government in improving housing, education, and amenities have also helped to influence key personnel in favour of transferring to Northern Ireland. Government policies have tended to make use of the advantages which Northern Ireland possesses, such as a surplus of suitable labour, and sites for factories with room for expansion, and to minimise the effects of the absence of fuel resources, or the expense of setting up a new factory away from the parent firm.

The engineering industry has benefited more than any other group from the Government's new industries policy. One problem has been that most of the new firms have been production units only of British, American, or European companies, and there has been the fear that in time of economic stress the factory in Northern Ireland would be closed rather than the main establishment. This has in fact happened, but on the other hand some firms have transferred all their production to Northern Ireland; the Government's policy has resulted in a diversification of the industry, and greatly increased employment. Northern Ireland cannot have any serious disadvantages as a location for the engineering industry, for otherwise the post-war expansion could not have taken place—for long-term operating costs are far more important than short-term Government assistance. On the other hand, the region does not have sufficient advantages for industry generally to enable production to expand to reduce unemployment to the level of the United Kingdom as a whole.

CHAPTER TEN

Resources

THE lack of raw materials in Ireland, especially the limited resources of coal and iron, did not become obvious until the industrial revolution; it was a long time, however, before public opinion became convinced of the realities of the situation. At the beginning of the nineteenth century Robert Fraser saw 'no reason to doubt that Ireland contained mineral productions which might afford employment to vast capitals'.[1] In 1860 it was suggested that 'the people of Ireland required only more knowledge of their own resources in order to guide them into a course of mercantile operations as would be at once safe and most profitable'.[2] Even at the beginning of the twentieth century it was necessary to remind people that 'popular notions of the vast mineral wealth of Ireland or her hidden coalfields waiting only for development were myths unworthy of a serious and reflective age'.[3]

Land

The greater security enjoyed by Ulster tenants enabled them to accumulate capital, and was largely responsible for the concentration of the linen industry in the north of Ireland. In the towns, however, it was often impossible, until the nineteenth century, to obtain long leases for industrial purposes. The Chichester family, later marquises of Donegall, owned the whole of Belfast from the seventeenth century, and it was their custom in the early days to grant leases for comparatively short terms, thus discouraging leaseholders from incurring much expense in the way of building. During the first fifty years of the nineteenth century the family got into financial difficulties and most of the tenants of the land on which Belfast now stands acquired perpetuity interests in their holdings. But for the financial plight of the Donegall family, the progress of Belfast might have been retarded, for previously their attitude had made improvements in the docks and water supply of the town almost impossible.[4] The availability of long leases was one of the chief factors which encouraged the rapid industrial growth of Belfast, especially the rapid expansion of the linen industry.

It has already been noted that suitable sites for shipyards on favourable terms, as well as good dry docks, encouraged the establishment and growth of shipbuilding in Belfast. The existence of an airport in Belfast was one of the attractions in setting up an aircraft factory. Sites for advance factories with room for expansion greatly assisted the Government's drive for new industry, especially when, after the second world war, engineering firms in Britain often found it impossible to expand beside their existing premises.

Iron

Up to the end of the sixteenth century, much of the iron used in Ireland was imported, but iron was also made locally on a small scale. In many areas bog iron ore underlying the peat could be obtained without difficult mining operations; it was suitable for making iron by the direct 'bloomery' process, so called because it produced small blooms of iron. The ore was reduced to its metallic state without the temperature being raised sufficiently to melt the metal; wrought iron was produced directly and the iron could not be cast in moulds, but the low temperature meant that the large phosphorous content of bog ore did not become a problem.

Harry Scrivenor, in his *History of the Iron Trade*, argued that until the time of Elizabeth I the wars in Ireland left the people with neither time nor inclination to search for iron mines,[5] and he implied that ironmaking was introduced from England at that time. In fact the wars to which Scrivenor refers would have made it essential for the Irish smiths to produce iron for weapons and defensive armour.

The new wave of colonists from Britain in the late sixteenth and early seventeenth centuries did, however, introduce into Ireland large-scale operations in the iron industry, as well as the capitalist organisation necessary for this scale of production. Instead of the old bloomery process they used the recently introduced blast furnace with bellows driven by water power, and the water-powered forge hammer for converting the pig iron from the furnace into wrought iron. The higher temperature reached in the blast furnace meant that bog iron ore could no longer be used, and a search for other types of iron ore began; these usually had to be obtained by mining, so Scrivenor may be correct in saying that the search for iron mines in Ireland did not begin until the time of Elizabeth I.

The new landowners found ironmaking a convenient way of exploiting their woodlands, and the insecurity of their position encouraged them to extract the maximum profit in the shortest possible time; they did not attempt to conserve their timber resources but used methods which produced cheap charcoal while rapidly destroying the woods. The clearing of the forests actually suited government policy in dealing with the native Irish by depriving them of places to hide. Cheap charcoal thus became available in Ireland when the iron trade in Britain was moving westward in search of cheap fuel; Ireland had few deposits of iron ore which could be smelted without admixture of other types, and much of the ore used in the blast furnaces was imported. The Irish iron industry owed its origin more to the availability of fuel than ore, as did the furnaces set up in the highlands of Scotland in the eighteenth century. The main centres of the charcoal iron industry in Ireland were in the south and west; in Ulster there were ironworks in the Lagan valley, to the north and west of Lough Neagh, around Lough Erne, and at a few other places such as Magheralin in county Down.[6]

Most of the northern furnaces appear to have been small, and bloomeries continued to be used in the north after the introduction of the blast furnace, possibly because they enabled local bog ore to be used.[7] Most of the Ulster ironworks were destroyed during the

1641 rebellion; many of them never resumed production, though some of those in the Belfast region were working in 1683, for in that year nearly 50 tons of iron 'all produced in the neighbourhood of the town' were exported from Belfast, while 310 tons of iron ore were imported from England,[8] hardly an indication of large-scale operations. In the eighteenth century the only charcoal ironworks in the north of Ireland appear to have been west of Lough Neagh, and the last of these closed in the late 1760s; in the south iron continued to be smelted with charcoal until the 1780s.

In the seventeenth century, most of the iron produced in Ireland was converted into malleable wrought iron bars and exported, mainly to Britain. The Irish demand for bar iron was limited, and largely confined to the maritime region remote from the ironworks, which was readily supplied from Britain. By the eighteenth century, the export market for Irish bar iron had largely disappeared, and the ironworks were forced to supply products more suitable for the local market, such as iron plates, nailers' rods, and cast-iron pots and pans.

The destruction of the woodlands eventually resulted in a shortage of charcoal which led to the closure of the ironworks. It is para-doxical that while locally produced iron was available in the north of Ireland until the 1760s, very little development of the iron-using trades took place, as there was only a limited market for finished goods within easy reach of the ironworks, yet about the time that the last charcoal blast furnace went out of production ironfoundries using imported materials began to be set up at the ports. The foundries used the recently developed cupola furnace and cheap pig iron made in Britain with coke.

Iron was not made with coke in Ulster; the ironworks at Arigna in Roscommon on the Connaught coalfield was the first in Ireland to smelt iron with coke. It was established in 1788 and operated at various times up to 1838 when the works were abandoned; it was said in 1852 that iron from Arigna had been 'extensively employed in the construction of the engines for which the eminent firm of

Victor Coates & Co of Belfast were justly celebrated',[9] but it is unlikely that much Arigna iron reached Belfast. The quality of the metal was generally agreed to be good, but the stormy history of the company would not have made it a reliable source of supply for the local engineering firms, and the transport costs from the works were considered to be very high.

In 1852, an ironworks using the hot blast process was opened at Creevelea in county Leitrim; the original owners went bankrupt in 1854, but the works continued to operate on a small scale until 1858, and unsuccessful attempts were made to smelt iron with processed peat.[10] There is no reason to think that the works supplied any appreciable quantities of iron to engineering firms in the north of Ireland.

Deposits of iron ore were discovered in county Antrim in the 1860s; these deposits do not appear to have been known in the seventeenth and eighteenth centuries, for the small charcoal ironworks then in operation on the Antrim coast imported their ore from Britain. In the 1870s, narrow-gauge railways were built to transport the ore to Larne or Belfast for export, but the boom was over by 1890; output was at its peak in 1880, and for several years thereafter the annual value was around £20,000. The Antrim ores, like most Irish iron ores, had disadvantages; they were not rich in iron and had an undesirably high content of phosphorus, aluminium, and titanium; they were used as a flux for the haematite ores of Cumberland but were not suitable for smelting alone. Demand gradually decreased, and by 1925 it was no longer profitable to export the Antrim ores except as ballast in ships returning empty to Britain. Mining was again undertaken during the second world war, but on a small scale, and was discontinued after a few years. Small deposits of iron ore occur elsewhere in the north of Ireland; most were exploited at one time or another but none were mined profitably for any length of time.

In the second half of the nineteenth century, the importance of local supplies of iron ore had decreased in Britain through the availability of cheap foreign ores, although it was still essential to have a good supply of fuel. The discovery of the Antrim ores raised hopes that Lisburn, Lurgan, or Portadown might be a suitable site for a furnace using Antrim ore and Tyrone coal; the Antrim ores, however, proved to be unsuitable for smelting alone, and Tyrone coal was being raised only in small quantities. The scale of operations in the iron industry increased, and by the beginning of the twentieth century the local demand in the north of Ireland would not have been sufficient to absorb the output of a single blast furnace.[11] Hopes of reviving the local iron industry gradually faded.

While it would not be true to say that there were no resources of iron in the north of Ireland, or that they were neglected in the periods of charcoal or coke smelting, for all practical purposes they might well not have existed for all the influence they had on the development of the engineering industry.

Although it was not possible to smelt iron economically in the area in the nineteenth century, it might still have been worthwhile to convert pig iron into malleable wrought-iron bars or such semi-manufactured products as plates, rods, and girders. To supply this type of market the Eliza Street Ironworks was established in Belfast in 1850, but it had three sets of proprietors in rapid succession, and none of them appear to have made the business a success. The last owners were the Belfast Iron Company, in which the moving spirit was Robert Hickson, a pioneer of iron shipbuilding at Belfast. When in 1853 Hickson embarked on iron shipbuilding, without being himself a practical shipbuilder, it was to secure a market for the output from the works. In addition to plates for boilers and ships the firm made wrought-iron beams and joists for warehouses; the venture, however, was a failure and the works closed in 1855. Wrought iron could be brought from England or Scotland more cheaply that it could be made at Eliza Street. It was suggested that the firm was started to work up iron scrap available in Belfast,[12] and this seems reasonable for it would have offered more hope of success than using imported pig iron. The expense of importing fuel must have been too great, for in the end it proved to be more profitable to export the scrap to Britain where coal was available.

Since it proved uneconomical to convert pig iron into wrought iron in the north of Ireland, there was little hope of establishing steelmaking on a commercial scale. The scarcity of local coal, and the limited demand for steel made it impossible to operate commercially in the area the large-scale methods of steelmaking which developed in the last quarter of the nineteenth century. With the substitution of steel for iron in shipbuilding, the imports of steel into Belfast increased almost tenfold between 1880 and 1900, but a large variety of steel products were used, none of which could have been produced locally on the optimum scale. In the 1950s, interest was aroused in the possibility of establishing a steel mill in the north of Ireland using an electric furnace to convert local supplies of scrap metal, but expert opinion considered that the scale of operations would be too small to be profitable.

Other Metals

In the development of the engineering industry, other metals were of much less importance than iron and steel. Amongst imports, lead was next in quantity, but was used more in the building trade than in engineering; copper and brass, though used in small quantities, were important in both engineering and shipbuilding. Small amounts of lead and copper were mined in the north of Ireland in the nineteenth century, but the ore was exported for smelting, and by the middle of the century the trade had ceased with the availability of cheaper foreign ores.

In county Antrim, bauxite, formerly known as alum clay, had been mined for many years before it began to be used for the production of aluminium; Antrim is the only area in the United Kingdom where it occurs in quantity. Mining was undertaken more systematically from 1873, and between 1882 and 1915 the total output amounted to some 300,000 tons. In 1896 works for the separation of alumina from bauxite were established at Larne by the British Aluminium Company; this was only the first stage in the production of aluminium, and the alumina was sent to Scotland where the metal was extracted by the electrolytic process. The local ore was not rich in aluminium and had a high silica content, and when more suitable ores became available the demand for Antrim bauxites declined; at the Larne works imported ores were used from the early 1930s. During the second world war, bauxite mining was revived and between 1942 and 1945 the output totalled some 300,000 tons. The production of alumina ceased at Larne in 1946, but the works continued in operation until 1960 for the recovery of red oxide for use as a pigment.

Deposits of other metals have been located in the north of Ireland but have not been exploited. In the 1960s interest was revived in the possibility of finding workable deposits of non-ferrous metals in the area, but it seems unlikely that these metals will be produced locally in sufficient quantity to influence the progress of the engineering industry. The Irish mines were most fully exploited from 1840 to 1880, and while it was often argued in Ireland that they were closed through pressure of competition by British producers, the crucial factors were the exhaustion of the most profitable deposits, and the discovery of cheaper and more abundant foreign sources of supply. In fact, much capital was lost in trying to develop mines in Ireland. Even when it was worth while to mine ores in Ireland it was seldom possible to smelt them economically, after charcoal ceased to be used, as the lack of cheap fuel in the area made the process uncompetitive.

Moulding Sand

The only raw material needed by the engineering industry which was readily available in the north of Ireland, particularly in the Belfast region, was foundry moulding sand. 'Belfast sand' was one of the constituents often included in sand mixtures for various

K

foundry purposes given in nineteenth-century textbooks. It was not a valuable material, and in 1913 the exports were reckoned to be worth only 2s 6d per ton,[13] but local supplies of moulding sand tended to reduce costs for the ironfounders.

Coal

The deposits of coal in Ireland are small and of little importance compared with those in Britain. Although the upper carboniferous strata cover a considerable part of the country, the coal-bearing beds have for the most part been denuded away, and only in a few isolated basins, or where they lie beneath newer deposits, have they been preserved. Most of the coal lies south of a line from Dublin to Galway; the two Ulster coalfields are at Ballycastle in Antrim, and in Tyrone. The Ballycastle coalfield is some 4 square miles in extent; most of the coal is to be found in the coastal areas, and outcrops are exposed in the cliffs. The deposits are of lower carboniferous age, or in other words, the coal measures proper in the region have been removed by denudation. There are ten seams of coal, but they are generally thin, and the accompanying rocks are mostly faulted and full of water; the one good seam, the 'main coal', some 4 ft in thickness, was largely worked out by the end of the eighteenth century.

It has been suggested that Ballycastle coal was mined as early as the thirteenth century, but extensive operations began only in the 1720s. In 1717, the Irish Parliament voted £1,000 to any person who would land 500 tons of coal at Dublin from any Irish port. Two Dublin merchants raised the stipulated 500 tons of coal at Ballycastle, and in 1721 obtained the reward; the following year they obtained a further £1,000 for bringing 5,000 tons of coal from Ballycastle. From 1723 to 1727 the Irish Parliament granted over £4,000 to the lessees of the Ballycastle mines, but the output was never large, and working appears to have been abandoned by 1730.

In 1736, Hugh Boyd secured a lease of the mines and obtained from the Irish Parliament grants of some £23,000 for developing coal mining and building a harbour; in the middle of the century 7,000 tons of coal were said to be shipped annually to Belfast, Drogheda, Dublin, and other ports. When Boyd died in 1765, his son took little interest in the mines or in the industries which his father had set up in Ballycastle, and by the 1780s very little coal was being mined, while the harbour had been damaged by storms and was silting up. In 1811, coal was still being mined at Ballycastle but only 30–60 tons were being raised weekly; the principal market was Coleraine, but some was sent to Ballymena and Antrim, and small quantities were carried inland for considerable distances to supply blacksmiths' forges. At the beginning of the nineteenth century, although the harbour was now useless, some coal was still being sent to salt works, limekilns, and bleach greens on the coast, but after 1831 no coal seems to have been despatched by sea, and in 1833 mining ceased.[14] Attempts have since been made from time to time to reopen the Ballycastle mines, but with little success; the most recent venture started in 1955 but came to an end in 1967.

The Tyrone coalfield covers some 12 square miles of coal measures proper; the easterly dip of the beds combined with numerous faults carries the coal to a great depth in a comparatively short distance from the outcrop, and hopes of finding a rich concealed coalfield to the east have not been fulfilled. The coal proved difficult to mine, mainly through the softness of the beds of coal, combined with the irregularity caused by faulting. Some coal was raised at Drumglass at the end of the seventeenth century, carted to Newry and shipped to Dublin, but it could not be sold at prices competitive with English and Scottish coal, so the enterprise was abandoned.

Throughout the eighteenth century there was continued interest in the possibility of supplying Dublin with Tyrone coal. Despite the construction of the canal from Newry to Lough Neagh and another from Lough Neagh to Coalisland, the coal trade did not develop, largely through lack of sound mining techniques and the squandering of substantial sums of public money provided to improve transport facilities.

At the beginning of the nineteenth century, instead of carrying coal to Dublin, barges were bringing English and Scottish coal to Coalisland for distribution there and farther inland. During the second quarter of the century, output improved, and coal was shipped to ports on Lough Neagh, and perhaps to Dublin; by road coal seldom reached customers beyond a 20 mile radius from the pits. The collieries were never really prosperous and in the nineteenth century large-scale operations were not undertaken. Tyrone coal production was insufficient to meet the needs of local industry when steam-driven machinery was introduced; it was used chiefly in distilleries and bleach greens, and for burning lime and bricks.

In the 1920s Sir Samuel Kelly undertook mining operations near Coalisland using modern methods and equipment; the first shaft was completed in June 1924 and the second a month later. There was provision for loading directly into railway waggons at the pit-head and no trouble was anticipated from flooding. Prospects for a substantial and regular output from the Tyrone coalfield at last seemed assured, but production suddenly ceased. The shafts had been sunk near a deep fault and when this was reached no further coal could be found; in the opposite direction the levels rose to the surface.[15] The colliery closed in 1926, and since then further investigations of the field have not indicated any possibility of mining coal economically on a large scale, although some mines in Tyrone were worked on a small scale in the 1930s and 1950s.

In the second half of the nineteenth century the Ulster mines produced about a tenth of the Irish coal output, then about 100,000 tons per annum. The whole of the Irish output would have been inadequate for the needs of the industries in the north of Ireland, for by the end of the century coal imports through Belfast alone exceeded a million tons per annum. In the 1930s and 1950s the total coal mined in the Tyrone coalfield and at Ballycastle seldom exceeded 5,000 tons a year. Coal mining in the north of Ireland had little influence on industrial development, and in particular had no effect on the progress of the engineering industry. Transport difficulties prevented coal from Ballycastle and Tyrone reaching Belfast and the provincial engineering centres in significant amounts when mining was at its peak; from the middle of the nineteenth century output was too limited and erratic to provide engineering firms with a reliable source of supply.

Peat

Deposits of peat are widely distributed in Ireland and have long supplied fuel satisfactory for domestic purposes. When little timber was left for making charcoal and resources of Irish coal proved to be limited, attention naturally turned to the possibility of using peat for industrial purposes. Charcoal made from peat had been used in prehistoric ironworking in Scotland and possibly in Ireland; up to the nineteenth century Irish smiths used it as a substitute for wood charcoal, and it was apparently satisfactory for work at the forge. Peat charcoal was occasionally used in larger-scale operations such as spade making, and it was suggested that it might be used to smelt iron ore or convert pig iron into wrought iron at the forge.

In 1751, Robert Rainey, who had an ironworks at Castledawson, claimed in a petition for financial assistance from the Irish Parliament that 'he had at great expense and after many experiments discovered a method of making compleat malleable iron from pig iron, by turf coal alone without any wood, by which there will be great saving to the nation'. He offered to make his methods public, and after a committee had looked into the matter, he was voted £300.[16]

When supplies of wood charcoal came to an end, some of the capital invested in the Irish ironworks might have been salvaged if peat could have been used for smelting. Two years after his first petition to the Irish Parliament, Rainey sought further assistance, claiming to have discovered 'the art of making pig metal with turf coal only, without any wood'. Again he was willing to instruct others in his methods, and again he was granted £300.[17] Rainey's efforts did not save the Irish iron industry, or even his own works which was for sale in 1755, together with a stock of 'turf and turf coal'.[18] His methods cannot have impressed local people, for when Martin Steel of Bellaghy proposed to reopen the ironfounding side of the business in 1758 he gave notice that he was willing to buy charcoal, but made no mention of buying peat or peat charcoal.[19]

In 1843 Nicholas Crommelin, proprietor of Newtowncrommelin in county Antrim, erected a furnace to smelt local ore with peat charcoal, but the process was not successful, and the furnace was soon abandoned. Unsuccessful attempts to smelt iron with peat were also made at Creevelea iron works in Leitrim, after the original proprietors who had used the coke hot blast process went bankrupt in 1854. Peat was not really suitable for use in the blast furnace, partly through its low mechanical strength, and attempts to use it for ironmaking in Britain were also unsuccessful, but apparently on the Continent it was used for metallurgical purposes up to the beginning of the twentieth century. In the north of Ireland peat has not been used to any great extent for raising steam for power; in the nineteenth century satisfactory methods of burning peat in furnaces had not been developed; in the twentieth century it became possible to use peat in electricity generating stations but the north of Ireland has not large supplies of readily accessible and easily worked peat like those of the Irish midlands, thus no turf-fired generating stations have been built in the north of Ireland.

Other Sources of Power

Water power was used in 1812 at works in Lisburn for making spindles and rollers for the textile industry, and some of the provincial engineering firms used water power, often to supplement other sources of power. In Belfast, water power was not available at the sites of most engineering works, and only one firm seems to have had its machinery driven by water; this was John Butler's works on the site of the old manor mill. The only firms consistently using water power were the country spade makers, who found water wheels quite suitable for driving their tilt hammers. Water wheels did not provide the steady and readily controlled output of power desirable for operating machine tools, and this, coupled with the uncertainty of the water supply, was the chief drawback in the use of water power in the engineering industry.

When it became obvious that local supplies of coal were unlikely to provide power for industry, much thought was devoted to discovering alternative sources of power. In 1866, it was suggested that as there were large supplies of limestone in Ireland and 'the Belfast chemists could produce sulphuric acid at three farthings a pound, if not cheaper, a "carbonic acid gas engine" might be useful in Ireland',[20] that is an engine driven by the carbon dioxide gas evolved by the reaction of sulphuric acid on limestone. Though ingenious, this was not a practical proposition. In the search for sources of cheap power no engineering firm in the north of Ireland appears to have imitated the marble polishing works in Galway, where the machinery in the 1840s was driven by the treadmill in the county gaol.[21]

The introduction of gas engines in the last quarter of the nineteenth century offered economies to the smaller engineering works, especially where intermittent running was required. The provision of public electricity supplies from the beginning of the twentieth century, combined with individual drives for machines, offered even greater flexibility and economy, but both gas and electricity were produced from imported fuels.

Transport of Raw Materials

As the north of Ireland had no useful resources of coal, iron, or other metals, and these had to be imported, costs of materials tended to be higher than in Britain; it does not follow, however, that costs everywhere in the north of Ireland were higher than everywhere in Britain. All through the nineteenth century, commentators in Ireland agreed that on the east coast raw materials could be obtained more cheaply than in many parts of Britain, particularly in London or in places depending on long hauls by road or rail. Belfast was fortunate in being able to obtain pig iron from the Clyde, where technical developments reduced costs, especially in the second quarter of the nineteenth century. The cheapness of bulk transport by sea from the Clyde and the north of England also helped to encourage the growth of shipbuilding at Belfast.

The Belfast shipbuilders occasionally benefited from the dumping of steel products by British or American steel producers, but only Harland & Wolff were large enough to secure their supplies of raw material by obtaining financial interests in steelmaking firms. The engineering firms in the provincial towns had to pay additional freight charges, but they were serving a local market protected to some extent from competition, and their competitors in Britain had to pay freight on finished goods.

In the early nineteenth century, coal cost four times as much in Belfast as in Leeds; by the middle of the century, with cheaper sea transport, the difference had practically disappeared. From the beginning of the nineteenth century the price of coal in Belfast compared favourably with that in London. Industries in Belfast were able to obtain coal at prices dearer than in the areas convenient to the coalfields, but not by any means the dearest in the United Kingdom. Farther inland, coal costs were higher and the average price for the north of Ireland as a whole would have been higher than the average for Britain. Even when coal was available from the Irish mines, it could not be delivered at Belfast or the other principal engineering centres as cheaply as imported coal.

In 1844 Sir Robert Kane estimated that the higher cost of coal in Ireland, in the case of the cotton industry, amounted to about half of 1 per cent of the total costs of production, and this might be offset by other costs being lower in Ireland, or by using coal less wastefully than in Britain.[22] There is some evidence that coal was used more efficiently in Belfast than in some centres in Britain; according to Alex B. Wilson in 1887, 'perhaps from the shrewdness of the millowners, more care was exercised in the economical production of steam power in Belfast than in any other town in the three kingdoms'. He produced figures to show that the cost per horse-power per annum for large steam engines was lower in Belfast than in London, Birmingham, or Glasgow.[23] If this is true, and Wilson's views have to be treated with respect for he was a designer of steam engines, it was achieved not by the use of special boilers or engines, but by the more efficient operation of conventional equipment; this would not have been difficult in view of the wasteful manner in which coal was used in Britain in the nineteenth century.

It was estimated that in 1935 for shipbuilding, marine engineering and electrical engineering the excess cost of coal in Northern Ireland as compared with Great Britain was 0·2 per cent of net output, and for mechanical engineering 0·1 per cent of net output.[24] These additional costs were amongst the lowest for Northern Ireland industries. After the second world war, coal costs in Northern Ireland continued to be higher than in Britain, and the Government of Northern Ireland introduced a fuel rebate to manufacturing industries to offset the higher cost of coal, although it was later extended to other fuels. It would be difficult to estimate how far this rebate has gone to reduce fuel costs in the engineering industry to parity with those in Britain, as the effects of the rebate vary from firm to firm.

Since the second world war, the engineering industry has come to depend more and more on public supplies of electricity, and by the late 1960s spent nearly as much on the purchase of electricity as on all other fuels combined. This has improved the competitive position of the industry for the charges for industrial electricity in Northern Ireland in the 1960s were roughly midway between the highest and the lowest rates charged in Britain, even before the effects of the fuel rebate scheme were taken into account.

The need to import coal and raw materials did not greatly hinder the development of the engineering industry, but reinforced the factors on the demand side which influenced the location of the industry and the products which could profitably be made. The importance of local supplies of coal and iron can be overrated and the significance of skill and enterprise overlooked. In the north of Ireland, however, the engineering industry developed in a region which not only lacked natural resources, but at the end of the eighteenth century was also poorly supplied with men skilled in metalworking and in organising the production and marketing of tools and machinery.

CHAPTER ELEVEN

The Labour Force

Engineering Crafts

At the beginning of the nineteenth century, despite the seeming availability of human resources as measured in terms of population, industrial labour in the sense of a stable, trained group, willing to work in factories, was scarce in the north of Ireland. The number of craftsmen in the area used to working metals and making machines was small, and the development of a skilled labour force was a slow process. It was significant that the rapid expansion of the engineering industry did not take place until the second half of the century, when the north of Ireland was able to benefit from the training of skilled labour in Britain.

When power-driven machinery was developed, it had to be constructed with the aid of the skills already available, especially those of the millwrights, carpenters, smiths, and clockmakers. By the middle of the nineteenth century, engineering crafts had generally assumed their modern form; the smiths continued to use their traditional skills, but the main bulk of the labour force was made up of new crafts. The patternmakers made models, mostly in wood, of articles to be cast in the foundry; the moulders prepared moulds in sand and poured the molten metal; the turners produced parts on the lathe, and the fitters assembled and erected the finished machinery.

Another craft developed during the industrial revolution, that of making boilers in heavy iron plate, and the boilermakers later undertook the building of iron and steel ships, as well as structural work in these materials. The sheetmetal workers carried on the skills of the tinkers and braziers, and their numbers in the engineering industry increased with the development of ventilating plant. There were many other small groups of specialist craftsmen, but the only important new craft to be introduced before the end of the nineteenth century was that of the electrical workers.

The development of new machine tools and processes led to greater specialisation and the evolution of semi-skilled occupations, while the introduction of more highly organised forms of production called for specialists such as draughtsmen, toolroom workers, technicians, ratefixers, and supervisors. These changes were not peculiar to the industry in the north of Ireland; the frequent interchange of workers between the area and Britain ensured that crafts and skills developed on the same pattern.

There was considerable resistance to factory work at the beginning of the industrial revolution, but no records have come to light of difficulties in recruiting workers for the engineering industry in the north of Ireland. In the countryside, the craftsman's standing may have been low if he had no land, so that farmers were reluctant to put their sons to a trade, but, as in Britain, the engineering workers were held in high esteem in the towns, and there was no shortage of recruits. After the potato famine not only were many workers compelled to leave the land, but many of those who served their needs were also thrown out of work, and engineering firms had no difficulty in recruiting the unskilled and semi-skilled workers who then formed at least a third of the labour force. A large number of women were employed in the linen industry, and there might have been difficulty in finding women workers if they had been required by the engineering industry. Few women, however, were employed by engineering firms in the north of Ireland before the second world war, and by then the demand for labour in the linen industry had begun to decline; engineering and shipbuilding were often regarded as complementary to textiles, the former employing men and the latter women, and giving a balance to the industrial labour force.

Mobility of Labour

During the nineteenth century, in Ireland as in Britain, unskilled workers seem to have moved usually only short distances in search of work, but many craftsmen had long been itinerant because they could not be supported permanently by the work available in any one district. The ironfounders, boilermakers, fitters, and turners were prepared to move from one engineering or shipbuilding centre to another looking for work, and in this they were encouraged by their trade unions in an endeavour to keep up wages by reducing the supply of labour in districts where work was scarce. This policy greatly increased the unions' bargaining power and helped to spread the membership of the national unions throughout the country; the 'tramping' system was the very backbone of some unions, such as the moulders.

From the 1890s, a permanent reservoir of unemployed existed at the main engineering centres, and employment was less likely to be obtained by travelling; conditions tended to be good or bad all over the country at the same time, and there was less hope of avoiding unemployment in one town by going to another. By that time, the labour force in the north of Ireland was well established, and local engineering firms were able to attract additional workers when required without the help of the tramping system which had been so valuable in the early stages. Mobility was also increased by cheap sea passages between Britain and the north of Ireland from the second quarter of the nineteenth century; indeed the local unions had to take strong action from time to time to keep workers from other areas out of Belfast, in order to avoid flooding the labour market and depressing the level of wages.

Belfast had attractions, especially for workers from Scotland, who found the small houses in Belfast more desirable than Glasgow tenements. Belfast benefited from experience elsewhere, and in the second half of the nineteenth century local bye-laws laid down

minimum housing standards which led to the building of small
houses that look dismal enough today, but at the time marked a
great improvement on what was available elsewhere. Early in the
century, overcrowding and insanitary conditions in some parts of
Belfast were as bad as anywhere, but these houses were mostly
cleared away after 1850. Living conditions in Belfast were probably
better than those the rural population and many inhabitants of the
provincial towns had to endure. At the Belfast meeting of the TUC
in 1893 Samuel Munro, President of the Belfast Trades' Council,
claimed that Belfast workers were better and more comfortably
housed than those of the majority of the large centres of industry.[1]
Belfast, however, was not a healthy town during the nineteenth
century; it was built on a flat site only a few feet above sea level, and
drainage was difficult. The drainage system was greatly improved at
the end of the century, and public health improved in consequence.
Belfast soon lost its dubious distinction of having one of the highest
death rates amongst the cities of the United Kingdom.

Belfast's reputation for recurrent political riots might have discouraged workers coming from other towns, but the importance of
this factor has perhaps been over-emphasised. Those coming from
Scotland would have been familiar with 'Orange and Green' tensions resulting from Irish immigration and pressure on employment;[2] indeed it has been suggested that these troubles were brought
to Belfast by shipyard workers from the Clyde.[3] This cannot be the
whole truth, for there had been religious riots in Belfast as early as
1813, long before there was any sizeable influx of Scottish shipyard
workers; their influence may, of course, have worsened the situation.
On the other hand the north of Ireland was generally free from the
agrarian outrages which characterised the struggle for the land in
the southern provinces, and industrial cities in Britain were not free
from riots in the nineteenth century, although their causes may have
been different and less enduring than those in Belfast. The factor
which helped to bring workers to Belfast, in spite of any doubts they
may have had about its public health and order, was the fairly

steady prosperity of the town from the 1880s to 1914, as far as shipbuilding and engineering were concerned; there were no severe or prolonged depressions such as occurred at many centres in Britain. After the first world war, Belfast was not so prosperous in comparison with cities in Britain, but it had still a powerful attraction for workers in the north of Ireland, and it has taken very determined efforts by the Northern Ireland Government to reverse the tendency for industry to concentrate in the city at the expense of the rest of the province.

Training

While many skilled workers came from Britain to live in the north of Ireland, others were trained locally, and it was natural that the British pattern of training should be adopted. An apprenticeship in engineering during the nineteenth century was a very unsatisfactory process of training; it was largely the apprentice's responsibility to learn what he could by watching and assisting journeymen. Few employers regarded it as their duty to make sure that apprentices gained a knowledge of all aspects of their craft, and semi-skilled workers were often left to gain experience as best they could, with little help from supervisors and craftsmen; the trade unions' main interest was in restricting the number of apprentices, in order to maintain the wage level of existing journeymen. In spite of the failure of employers and unions to encourage more effective forms of training, a high standard of skill was attained because the industry was able to attract a large proportion of intelligent men who were willing to study in their own time to complete their training.

Few institutions to provide theoretical training in engineering, to supplement practical experience on the job, were formed in the north of Ireland before the end of the nineteenth century. Like their counterparts in Britain, the local Mechanics' Institutes were forced to provide elementary classes in general education rather than in science and technology, and by 1850 they had largely ceased to attract mechanics and approximated to literary and philosophical societies for a mainly middle-class clientele. In the last quarter of the century some evening classes were held at the Belfast Working Men's Institute and Temperance Hall, at the technical school in Hastings Street, which catered chiefly for the textile trade, and at the Belfast Model School, but by 1900 the total enrolment in these institutions, together with the Government sponsored school of art, was only about 800. Some financial help was given by the Science & Art Department and by the City & Guilds of London Institute, but it was not until public money became available for technical education that further progress was made.[4]

In the last decades of the nineteenth century, increasing foreign competition directed attention to the deficiencies of technical education in the United Kingdom as compared with the Continent and America. In 1890, 'whiskey money' from local taxation was made available for technical education in Britain, but in Ireland it was devoted to primary and secondary education, partly because until 1898 there were no county councils to administer technical education. In 1896, the Recess Committee felt that the only good practical education which could be obtained in Ireland was in the reformatory and industrial schools for 'the children of the criminal and improvident classes'.[5]

Largely as a result of the recommendations of the Recess Committee, the Department of Agriculture & Technical Instruction for Ireland was set up in 1899; a system of technical education was established which penetrated the whole country, and technical schools were provided in practically every large town, so that even today classes are available in towns which, were they situated in Britain, would still be without such facilities. Instruction was still confined to the principles of science and art applicable to industries, and was shaped by the examination requirements of ambitious students, rather than the needs of industry; but the improvements in technical education in the north of Ireland during the first decade of the twentieth century were impressive.

There were further developments in the 1920s and 1930s, but rapid progress was not made until after the second world war with the introduction of day release and block release schemes, as well as training schools for apprentices in individual firms. As part of the drive for new industry, facilities for retraining craftsmen and training semi-skilled workers were provided in Government training centres, and schemes were also established for training workers in the premises of new and expanding firms. In 1964, the Northern Ireland Engineering Industry Training Board was set up to co-ordinate and improve training for all grades in the industry, and to spread the cost of training more equitably; the Board has attempted to forecast manpower needs and to plan training accordingly. Northern Ireland has devoted proportionately more money and effort to training and retraining than Britain, and as manpower is the province's main resource this is sound policy.

Wages

At the beginning of the nineteenth century, when engineering skills were scarce, earnings were high in Belfast; at the Lagan Foundry in 1812 skilled workers could earn as much as 40s a week.[6] By 1836, the level of earnings appears to have fallen, and the 'better sort of mechanics' in Belfast were said to earn only 20s a week;[7] in the 1870s the wage rate in Belfast had increased to 30s, and by 1914 had reached 41s. Rates in Belfast increased from 1860 to the end of the century more rapidly than in most other engineering centres, and by 1910 the fitters' rate was the highest in Ireland, and in the United Kingdom was exceeded only by the rates in London, south Wales, and Sheffield.[8] The position was similar for other skilled trades, whose wage rates usually followed closely any variations in the fitters' rate. In the provincial towns, the wage rates were lower than in Belfast, but by no means the lowest in the United Kingdom.

The wage rate, the minimum payment recognised by employers and unions for a full week's work, was not necessarily the same as

L

the amount workers actually earned each week; this could be reduced by short-time working or increased by overtime, piecework,
and the payment of special allowances. While Belfast wage rates
rose to be among the highest in the United Kingdom, the average
earnings of engineering workers in the city were generally below the
national average. The comparative prosperity of Belfast from the
1880s, combined with strong trade union organisation, tended to
increase wage rates. On the other hand, there was little repetitive
work which lent itself to piecework payments in the branches of
engineering practised in Belfast, and therefore little opportunity to
supplement earnings; although Belfast was relatively prosperous,
the rate of expansion in engineering was much less than in Britain,
so there was not the same tendency for earnings to drift upwards as
at the larger British engineering towns.

The differential between the rates for skilled men and labourers
was much greater in the north of Ireland than in Britain up to 1914.
This was characteristic of wages all over Ireland, at least from the
beginning of the nineteenth century; skilled men could often earn
three times as much as labourers. There was chronic underemploy-
ment in Ireland, and the influx of cheap labour from the country
into the towns forced down labourers' wages, but skilled labour was
scarce and wages in consequence little different from those in Britain; men with a skilled trade could readily find employment in
Britain or overseas if they were not well enough paid in Ireland. As
the wages of semi-skilled workers were related to those of labourers
rather than skilled men, it was probable that they were lower in the
north of Ireland than in Britain in the nineteenth century.

Engineering firms in the north of Ireland may have found some
advantage in having large numbers of men in the area willing to
undertake unskilled and semi-skilled work at a level of wages lower
than in Britain. The industry did not depend on cheap labour as far
as skilled men were concerned; time rates of wages were high, and
if earnings were lower than in Britain, the main reason was the
absence of piecework to supplement wages. The employers would,

no doubt, have been glad to introduce piecework systems if their methods of production had favoured them, for while the effect was to increase the workers' earnings, the main object was to reduce unit costs to the employer. Until 1914, the engineering unions were well satisfied with the high wage rates and the absence of piecework schemes outside shipbuilding in the north of Ireland. Indeed in 1861, in reply to a union inquiry as to whether piecework was operated in Belfast, the local secretary of the Amalgamated Society of Engineers replied: 'None, God be thanked!'[9]

The introduction of wage negotiations at national level during the first world war did not help to iron out earnings differentials between grades or between districts in the United Kingdom, for bargaining also continued at works level and systems of payment by results permitted earnings to increase, especially in districts where the industry was prosperous. The time rate of wages lost its importance, and by the 1960s few workers in the industry received only the minimum rate; while time rates in Northern Ireland continued to be high, this was no longer significant; much more important was the fact that average earnings did not attain the same level as in Britain.

Earnings in Northern Ireland fell further behind those in Britain in the late 1920s, and in the 1930s remained 10–20 per cent lower than in Britain. Northern Ireland earnings caught up with the national average in the early 1940s, pushed up by the greatly increased activity due to war work, especially the long hours of overtime, but declined again after the war. In the early 1950s, earnings were again not far below the national level, but decreased again to some 85 per cent of the average for Britain. The averages for both Britain and Northern Ireland conceal wide differences in earnings between areas or firms in the same area, and between grades within the same firm; while earnings in Northern Ireland have been generally lower than in Britain, the province has not always been the lowest-paid engineering region in the United Kingdom.

There appear to be two main reasons for the differential in earnings between Britain and Northern Ireland. Firstly, the weekly hours worked in Northern Ireland were generally less than in Britain, and this reduced total earnings. In 1961, average weekly earnings in engineering and shipbuilding in Northern Ireland were some 83 per cent of the average for Britain; hourly earnings, however, were over 88 per cent of the British average.[10] Secondly, in the north of Ireland there has not been the continuing excess demand for labour which characterised some regions in Britain, and therefore less tendency for earnings to drift upwards. It was not only in the engineering industry that earnings were lower than in Britain, but in this trade earnings approached the British levels more closely than in most manufacturing industries. The lower level of earnings, however, has not attracted sufficient industry to reduce unemployment to the same level as in Britain.

There is some evidence that in the nineteenth century unemployment in engineering in the north of Ireland was rather less than in many centres in Britain, but since the 1920s the position has been reversed. The level of unemployment in the engineering industry in Northern Ireland since the 1940s has been less than the average for the province, but in shipbuilding the unemployment level has occasionally been much higher than the local average.

While workers in the Northern Ireland engineering industry have usually not had as high earnings as their counterparts in Britain, their normal working week, holidays, and other conditions of employment have generally been the same as in the rest of the United Kingdom. It was not until the 1920s that working conditions were regulated by national agreements, but before that they were practically the same as in Britain, largely because the local trade unions and employers' associations were part of larger organisations covering the whole of the United Kingdom.

Industrial Relations

The engineering workers do not appear to have been involved in the labour unrest and violence which characterised many Irish industries early in the nineteenth century. Their industry, unlike many others, was expanding, and as they were few in number their skills were in demand, so they would have had no need to take violent action to secure a hearing for their claims. In the middle of the century there was some friction, for the Belfast secretary of the ironmoulders and several union members were in gaol for conspiracy in 1852, as the result of a strike.[11]

From the 1860s, labour relations in engineering in the north of Ireland were generally good; this contributed to the growth of the industry by enabling firms to meet delivery dates and so retain the goodwill of customers. The contrast between the life and prospects of the Belfast workers and those of the agricultural labourers in the less prosperous parts of Ireland may have made the engineering workers more content with their lot. It is more likely that the religious tensions within the community and the home-rule controversy diverted attention from chartism, syndicalism, guild socialism, and militant trade unionism generally. This was not, as James Connolly thought, the result of a deliberate policy by the local employers,[12] but part of the political situation which tended to bind groups of workers and employers together in the face of those whom they regarded as common enemies.

The engineering industry developed some fifty years later than in Britain, and thus benefited from the mistakes in industrial relations made there in the early years. As there was no legacy of bitterness there was less antipathy between unions and employers than in many other industrial centres; the Belfast employers appear to have made no attempt to destroy trade unions in the 1860s and 1870s when this was being attempted in Britain, and later they refused to recruit strike-breakers from the National Free Labour Association and consistently declined to give financial assistance to that organisation. The good industrial relations in the north of Ireland were not the result of weakness or lack of policy on either side, for the employers and unions were amongst the best organised in the

United Kingdom, and the percentage membership of organisations on both sides was, and has remained, well above the average.

Branches of what became the national engineering unions were established in the north of Ireland in the first half of the nineteenth century. The moulders had a branch in Belfast in 1820, and the boilermakers in 1841; when the Amalgamated Society of Engineers was formed in 1851 branches of the constituent unions already existed in Belfast, Londonderry, and Newry. Branches of the other craft unions were formed from the 1870s to the 1890s, and while a number of small local engineering unions existed, they were absorbed by the larger unions by the 1920s.

In the 1890s unskilled workers, especially in the shipyards, began to be recruited into membership of the general unions, but unions for draughtsmen, technicians, and clerical workers did not gather strength until the second quarter of the twentieth century. Most unions regarded their Belfast branches as amongst their strongest, and the percentage of union members there amongst the highest in the United Kingdom; trade union organisation in the provincial towns, however, was more sporadic until after the second world war.

In 1866, at a time when employers' organisations were still novelties, trade union activity in Belfast was sufficient to persuade the employers to set up an association of their own. At a meeting in the Belfast Museum on 25 May 1866 the Belfast Engineers', Ship Builders', Founders', & Machine Makers' Association was formed for 'mutual support in obtaining information and resisting unreasonable demands from workmen'. The chair was taken by E. J. Harland, and all the larger engineering firms were represented. At first the association confined itself to obtaining information from members and from correspondents in other districts; it did not negotiate directly with the unions, but advised members on how to deal with disputes. No doubt the member firms were chary of outside interference, even by their own association, which was prohibited by its rules from 'interfering with their individual will'. The committee, however, had a powerful aid to discipline as members could be fined substantial sums for disregarding their advice.[13] In 1872, the first direct negotiations between the association and the 'workmen's association' took place on a claim for a reduction in the working week to fifty-four hours. The workmen's association on this occasion consisted of two representatives from each firm and appears to have been an *ad hoc* joint committee rather than an established federation of unions.

In 1885 the association was reconstituted as the Belfast Employers Association for Engineers, Shipbuilders, Founders, Machine Makers & Other Trades, and it was confined to employers of skilled labour. There was difficulty in catering for so many interests in one association, and in 1896 the rules were amended to divide the association into seven sections, and most members enrolled in more than one. This, in part, satisfied the shipbuilders who had objected to the up-town employers voicing opinions on purely shipbuilding matters, and removed the objection by the ironfounders that they could be out-voted by the shipbuilders. From the 1890s conferences with craft unions became common, and from 1896, in spite of the rules, negotiations were not restricted to unions for skilled workers. The association did not concern itself with price fixing, but confined its attention to questions relating to the employment of labour; this was perhaps a matter of practical politics rather than of deliberate policy. From time to time suggestions were made that price lists should be drawn up; member firms, however, were engaged in such diverse forms of engineering that they were of little practical value. The ironfounders' section spent some time discussing prices for castings; this was the only branch of the industry where a large number of firms produced similar products, and where price fixing was for a time practicable.[14] The association has continued in existence and is therefore one of the oldest engineering employers' associations in the United Kingdom. Although its name was changed from the Belfast Employers' Association to the Engineering Employers' Northern Ireland Association, it was not until after the second world war that it attracted large numbers of engineering firms outside Belfast.

The National Federation of Shipbuilders & Engineers of the United Kingdom was formed in 1889; it originated on the Clyde, and the Belfast employers' association became affiliated, but in 1890 the engineering firms retired from the federation, leaving it to the shipbuilders. In 1895, a joint committee was set up between the Glasgow, Greenock, and Belfast employers' associations, at the suggestion of the Clyde associations, to deal with a wage claim by shipwrights. When a similar claim was put forward by the members of the Amalgamated Society of Engineers, further joint action was proposed by the Belfast association; negotiations with the union broke down and the Belfast men went on strike, thereupon 25 per cent of the Clyde members of the union were locked out. This precipitated a strike which continued for sixteen weeks and was terminated in Belfast only when the union executive directed their members to return to work, and withdrew their benefits. The movement towards federation of the employers' associations led to a meeting at Carlisle on 27 November 1895 attended by representatives from Belfast, Barrow, the Clyde, and the north-east coast of England, and in 1896 the Employers' Federation of Engineering Associations was formed with headquarters in Glasgow.

The dispute which arose in the following year over a claim for a reduction in the working week in London spread rapidly over the country and resulted in a national lock-out of engineering workers from July 1897 to February 1898. A side effect of the dispute was the rapid growth of Federation membership; the title of the federation was eventually changed to the Engineering Employers' Federation and the head office transferred to London.

The dispute was regarded by employers as an attempt by the unions to gain control over their workshops, and by the unions as an organised effort by the employers to destroy the unions;[15] the original cause of the dispute soon receded into the background and discussion ranged over freedom of employment, piecework, overtime, rating of workmen and manning of machines, and apprentices, as well as the demand for a forty-eight hour week. Although the immediate aims of the unions were defeated, the settlement after the lock-out resulted in national recognition of the negotiating rights of the engineering unions, and the establishment of the first national procedure for dealing with disputes.

The formation of the federation led to the resignation of Harland & Wolff from the Belfast Employers' Association. The association understood that the other partners in the firm wished to remain in the federation, but Lord Pirrie refused, as he could not dominate it. This placed Workman Clark in a delicate position, as they did not wish to offend Lord Pirrie; they eased the situation by resigning from the local association though not from the federation. In 1897, during the lock-out, Lord Pirrie was Mayor of Belfast, and in a speech on 14 December he criticised the employers' tactics, arguing that they were fifty years out of date. This brought from the local association a tart rejoinder, reminding him that his firm had been instrumental in founding the federation, that the lock-out on the Clyde in 1895 had been mainly for the benefit of his firm, and that he had withdrawn from the federation partly because it had not gone far enough in locking-out all the engineering trades.[16] This naturally did not reconcile Lord Pirrie with his fellow employers, and not until after his death did the marine engineering firms rejoin the federation, but as a separate association, the Belfast Marine Engineering Employers Association.

The inclusion of the north of Ireland in the British system of industrial relations involved the region in the disputes of the 1890s, in the managerial functions lock-out of 1922 which came at a time of political unrest in Ireland, and in the national wage disputes following the second world war, but generally it was a stabilising influence. There were advantages in having local disputes referred for consideration by the national organisations of employers and unions. The close association with British institutions was perhaps inevitable in view of the constant interchange of workers between the two countries.

Both workers and employers in the engineering industry in the north of Ireland played a full part in national movements, but the industrial relations in the area continued to be good. Firms in Northern Ireland have had more conferences with trade unions in proportion to numbers employed than in Britain, but in the 1960s, at least, fewer and shorter disputes. As in the nineteenth century, this has helped the growth of the industry, and since the second world war engineering has shown the greatest growth in employment of all local manufacturing industries.

CHAPTER TWELVE

Finance and Enterprise

Early Sources of Capital

FOR most of the nineteenth century, the capital required to set up engineering works in the north of Ireland was provided, as elsewhere, by the owners themselves, aided by loans from their relatives and friends, by mortgages on their property, and by entering into partnerships with men of wealth; most firms were built up slowly from small beginnings by the reinvestment of profits. The founder of the firm had to find the capital, shoulder the risks of the enterprise, and obtain orders and credit, as well as undertake the practical management of the works; his personal ability, character, and business connections were all important.

Little capital had been required by the independent metal craftsmen, but when engineering works were established in the nineteenth century, with a foundry and expensive machine tools, the position had changed; the capital needed increased rapidly, and while in 1825 a maker of textile machinery had to spend only about £50 on tools, by 1841 he had to invest some £1,000.[1] There were considerable variations in the amounts of capital required; the Reynolds brothers started with £50, but E. J. Harland had to borrow £5,000 to take over the Queen's Island shipyard. The engineering industry did not grow out of the small metal crafts of the area, so there was no class of capitalists organising outworkers and later setting up engineering works. There were no local ironmasters or landowners accustomed to encourage industry in order to expand the output of their furnaces or mines, and the linen industry does not appear to have invested heavily in engineering.

Capital seems to have been accumulated largely within the engineering industry itself; the early firms were set up by men who had accumulated both capital and experience in Britain, and subsequently new firms were established by those who had been trained and had built up some savings in the old engineering works.

Limited Liability

There appear to have been no joint stock companies in engineering in the north of Ireland until the introduction of limited liability. Until this was done, there was no easy way of mobilising the capital of those who wished to invest but were unwilling to undertake the liabilities of partnership in businesses about which they might know very little. From 1782 Ireland, in theory at least, had an advantage over Britain in this respect, for an Act of the Irish Parliament of that year permitted partnerships with limited liability. A firm could take 'anonymous partners' not liable for the debts of the partnership beyond the amount they originally subscribed. The restrictions placed on these partnerships made them difficult to operate; they had to be registered and return a yearly statement of accounts, they were limited to fourteen years duration with a capital between £1,000 and £50,000, but, more important, the anonymous partners could not withdraw more than half of their yearly profits, and interest, therefore, became a serious burden on the general partners. In spite of their disadvantages, limited partnerships were used in Belfast from the 1780s until about 1815 to mobilise local capital for the cotton, linen, brewing, distilling, and other industries of the town.

In 1785, for instance, £1,300 in shares of £100 was raised by a group of Belfast men, mostly merchants, to set up a glass works, an indication that there were in the town men willing and able to invest if they had security.[2]

Limited partnerships were not adopted in engineering, but from the 1850s limited company organisation was used, as in Britain, to confer added protection on the existing partners in family firms, rather than to attract new capital. In a few cases limited companies were formed to take over long-established works when the owners got into financial difficulties, instances being John Rowan & Sons Ltd and the Newry Foundry Co Ltd. By the middle of the twentieth century practically all engineering works were owned by limited companies, but only a few of the locally based firms had become public companies. The majority of the new firms from Britain and overseas were public companies, but little of their capital was raised in Northern Ireland.

Banking and Credit

The linen industry not only provided a market for engineering firms but also, with the provision trade, laid the foundations of banking and credit in the north of Ireland; this was of great assistance in the expansion of the engineering industry and in the development of its overseas markets.

At the beginning of the eighteenth century the name of Belfast 'appeared in the first rank in the scale of credit of the commercial towns of Europe, and on the exchange of Amsterdam'.[3] The fact that the linen trade imported flax from Europe and exported linen to Britain facilitated engineering firms in exporting machinery to Europe and in buying raw materials in Britain.

Most trade up to 1914 was financed by bills of exchange circulating freely not only in the United Kingdom but also in Europe; it was important that bills drawn or endorsed in Belfast should circulate readily, and that Belfast firms should be able to find bills drawn in Britain to pay their suppliers, while those who bought machinery should be able to find bills acceptable in Belfast. The collection of bills when due became very important, and as it was a specialised business, firms were established in Belfast by the middle of the eighteenth century to discount bills.

There were few private banks in the north of Ireland, but they were financially sound and there were none of the failures which characterised private banking in the south. When the formation of joint stock banks became possible in 1825, three were established in Belfast in quick succession, and a fourth in 1836, and branches were soon opened throughout the north of Ireland. In 1832, J. R. Mc-Culloch regarded the collection of bills as the greatest service provided by banks, and although they also offered a useful service in making payments for customers, giving information on the credit worthiness of clients, and acting as safe deposits, lending money was not then regarded as one of their main functions.[4]

Most manufacturers started with a credit balance at their bank for making payments to suppliers, and used their account for the deposit of cash; it was only after they had built up the business with their own resources that they could rely on the banks for part of their trading capital. The banks lent cautiously in Ireland, but this was the result, not the cause, of the lack of economic progress. Many small farmers would have been able to make good use of loans if they had had security of tenure; there was no shortage of people with schemes for the solution of Irish problems, there was, however, a shortage of sound, profitable enterprises to which the banks could lend their depositors' money with security.

In the north there were few complaints of lack of credit; there the joint stock banks operated the Scottish 'cash credit' system, which permitted a trader in need of capital to open an account on which he could draw up to a fixed amount, interest being charged only on the outstanding balance. This system was a potent influence in the commercial development of the north of Ireland, as it was in Scotland, up to the end of the nineteenth century.[5] The banks continued to make only short-term loans to finance particular operations, leaving the provision of risk capital to other institutions.

Supply of Capital

Complaints were often made of the lack of capital in Ireland, and suggestions made for Government action to remedy the situation; the shortage of capital, however, was more apparent than real and was a symptom rather than a cause of the economic difficulties in Ireland. In 1798, Thomas Wallace pointed out that 'the want of capital in Ireland was more frequently complained of than felt', for 'the style of living of the upper and middle classes indicated no lack of money', and he noted that the newspapers carried many advertisements offering substantial sums to be lent on good personal security.[6]

The flow of money from Ireland for investment elsewhere could not have taken place if there had actually been a shortage of capital, and although the Irish banks were slow to lend money this was not because they had none to lend. In Belfast, there appears to have been no difficulty in raising capital when there was a sound project to finance; when the Ulster Railway was seeking £600,000 capital in 1836, the £50 shares were taken up quickly in Belfast and the north of Ireland, as well as in Manchester, Liverpool, and Dublin.[7] Again at the beginning of the twentieth century, when the Falls Foundry in Belfast became part of Fairbairn Lawson Combe Barbour Ltd, numerous small investors in the north of Ireland became shareholders.

Since the opportunities for profitable investment in Northern Ireland are less in proportion to the level of savings than in Great Britain, funds tend to flow to Britain for investment. In recent years, attempts have been made to channel Northern Ireland funds into local industry and to attract investment from outside the province, by setting up an issuing house and a number of commercial organisations to provide finance for local business. The Northern Ireland Government has given financial assistance to new and expanding industries through loans and grants, but has not as yet accepted the frequently repeated suggestion that a Government-backed industrial development finance corporation should be established, which would provide risk capital for new enterprises.

While there has been extensive investment since the 1950s by new firms from Britain and overseas, Northern Ireland still lacks capital in the sense that there are not enough openings for profitable investment to yield full employment. As in the past, the difficulty is not an absolute lack of capital; in 1962 evidence was given to the Hall Committee that no enterprise in Northern Ireland, requiring capital, and able to show prospects of earning a reasonable level of profits, found greater difficulty in raising funds than did firms in Britain.[8]

Profits

No one would have set up an engineering works in the north of Ireland if he had not expected to make a profit. There were suggestions that the level of profits was higher in Ireland than in Britain in the nineteenth century,[9] partly through the greater insecurity of investments; there was certainly no suggestion that capitalists in the north of Ireland might have to accept lower profits than their counterparts in Britain because of the natural disadvantages of the region.[10] There was little to impede the flow of capital between Ireland and Britain, and it is unlikely that money would have been invested in engineering firms in the north of Ireland if higher profits could have been earned by investing the money in Britain.

Once engineering works were in existence it might have been sound economics to continue operations if profit levels fell temporarily below those in Britain; if there had been a substantial difference over a long period, engineering could hardly have continued in the area, and it would certainly have been impossible for the industry to expand by attracting capital from outside the province, or by financing the expansion out of profits.

From 1873, the 'Great Depression' led to a fall in profit levels in the United Kingdom as a whole, and about this time some of the longer-established engineering firms in the north of Ireland began to get into financial difficulties, and later some of them went out of business. It is impossible to be certain whether this was due to a fall in profits to an uneconomic level, to stiffer competition and the failure to keep abreast of technical developments, or simply to a decline in the efficiency of management such as led to the closure of firms in Britain which had once been prominent in the engineering industry.

In the twentieth century, the industry has become greatly diversified, and as it includes subsidiaries of companies from Britain and overseas, it would be difficult to assess the level of profits for the industry as a whole. Indications are, however, that in the early 1960s British firms which established branches in Northern Ireland found that the rate of return on capital invested in the province was at least as high as at the parent works in Britain.[11]

Enterprise

The significance of physical capital for industrial growth can be overestimated; the capacity to create wealth depends on people, and in the absence of other natural advantages the growth of the engineering industry in the north of Ireland must be explained in human terms.

Few of the early engineering works in the north of Ireland were established by local men; Job Rider, John Hind, Stephen Cotton, George Horner, and E. J. Harland came from England, James Combe and James Mackie from Scotland. From the middle of the nineteenth century, however, local men trained in the original works began to set up in business for themselves or to take over the management of existing firms when founders retired or got into financial difficulties.

It was to be expected that engineering techniques would be introduced into the north of Ireland from Britain. It was only in Britain that conditions were favourable for the beginning of the industrial revolution in the second half of the eighteenth century, and techniques developed there were used on the Continent, in America, and throughout the world. The traffic was not all in one direction, for

M

as soon as engineering had been firmly established in the north of Ireland, new ideas emerged which contributed to the advancement of engineering generally.

The men who created the engineering industry were practical engineers; even in the relatively prosperous north of Ireland the landowners did nothing to help the development of engineering, and little assistance was forthcoming from the linen or other local industries. Those who became partners in the early engineering works, without being themselves engineers, were few in number and had little in common.

When Victor Coates joined the firm which owned the Lagan Foundry, he was a hairdresser with premises in Castle Street,[12] and he continued taking orders for the foundry at his hairdressing establishment until, on the death of Edward Stainton, he found himself in control of the business. He was obviously a man of ability and enterprise, but it is nevertheless surprising that, with his background, he was able to carry on the ironfounding business and develop steam-engine making.

William Dunville, who was James Combe's original partner in the Falls Foundry, was a local whiskey distiller; he appears to have been made a partner for his wealth, not his engineering knowledge, and later the active partners in the firm were Barbours from the linen thread trade, relations of the Combes by marriage. In contrast with many enterprises which failed in the south because they were set up by men with capital but no business experience, the engineering firms in the north of Ireland were started by practical engineers, backed in some cases by local men with business experience as well as wealth. It seems clear that the early entrepreneurs were attracted to the north of Ireland, not by the local market for small metal goods, but by the opportunity to exploit new techniques such as ironfounding, the making of steam engines and textile machinery, and the provision of a machinery repair service. Once a skilled labour force had been built up, and local men had been trained so that they could undertake the management of engineering works, it became possible for further types of equipment to be designed and produced.

Belfast had one of the earliest co-operative retail stores, established in 1830,[13] but there were no co-operative enterprises in engineering, although the unions, in theory at least, were in favour of the extension of co-operative production. In 1884 a co-operative foundry was started by the Dublin moulders, but apparently without success;[14] nothing similar appears to have been attempted in the north of Ireland.

Although the Northern Ireland Government has done a great deal to encourage the expansion of industry, political opinion has not favoured public enterprise in manufacturing industry. It was perhaps an historical accident that the British Government found itself as majority shareholder in Short Brothers & Harland, and this does not seem to have created a distinctive policy for the company. Amongst public authorities, only those engaged in transport became involved in engineering production; the most enterprising was the Ulster Transport Authority, which did pioneering work in the application of diesel traction to railway working.

Up to 1914 there were in the north of Ireland many capable engineers who kept in close touch with current developments in engineering; some of them were at the forefront of rapidly developing sections of the industry. While in the 1920s and 1930s little progress was made, this was not because the region suddenly found itself without men of enterprise; local economic conditions forced men like Harry Ferguson to go to Britain or overseas to have their inventions put into production successfully. With the increase in the scale of production, in some sections of the industry the days of starting on a small scale have gone; this is one reason why most of the large new firms established since the second world war have been branches of established engineering firms in Britain, America, or Europe. In many fields it has become increasingly difficult for entrepreneurs anywhere to commence production successfully without very substantial investment both on the technical and commercial sides. The diversification of the industry, however, has created new opportunities for local men to provide services for the larger firms, and a number of small firms have been set up to supply new products to the local market. As in the previous century, the introduction of new techniques has acted as a catalyst to local enterprise, and if the expansion of the engineering industry has not been as great as the available labour force would have permitted, the expansion was retarded not by lack of enterprise but by the lack of sufficient profitable opportunities to apply it.

Organisation

There was in the north of Ireland no direct link between the independent metal craftsmen of the eighteenth century and the engineering works of the nineteenth century; there were no out-workers to be persuaded to work in factories. Capitalist organisation was introduced, ready developed, by those who set up the early ironfoundries, and the region was kept in touch with progress in industrial organisation in Britain not only by the political union of the two countries but also by periodic infusions of new blood from the British engineering industry.

In the nineteenth century, the owner or partners in an engineering works had to provide the technical knowledge to originate and design the products, organise efficient purchasing and production, sell the finished goods and keep in touch with market developments, plan to keep ahead of competitors, raise money to finance production and expansion, and shoulder all the risks of the enterprise. It is not surprising that some, such as the Rowan brothers, who were brilliant engineers, did not have the commercial ability to make a success of their business, and that others were able to make a good beginning but not to continue successfully.

In the large firms the chief partners divided the duties between them. In Harland & Wolff, from 1874 when W. J. Pirrie and Walter H. Wilson became partners, until the death of E. J. Harland in

1895, the four men made a remarkably efficient team: Harland was the inventive genius, Wolff the financier, Wilson the practical naval architect, and Pirrie the businessman and salesman, but all were able engineers who could, and did, undertake each other's work when necessary.[15]

In the firms making textile machinery there was similar specialisation, one partner managing the works and another spending much of his time travelling in search of orders. The smaller firms, especially those in the provincial towns, suffered from having too few active partners to attend to all the functions of management efficiently. When limited liability organisation was adopted it was used largely to confer added protection on the existing members of the family firm; the women of the family, who took little active part in the running of the works, replaced those who earlier in the century lent money on mortgages or personal security.

Until 1914, family companies were perhaps a source of strength and flexibility, for one essential for success was the ability to change methods and products quickly when necessary. In more recent times they have in some cases been a disadvantage, providing limited enterprise, failing to attract investment, and perpetuating narrow specialisation, but some family firms have continued to show evidence of great enterprise and adaptability. The introduction of new firms from outside Northern Ireland has helped to improve industrial organisation by popularising new techniques of production and management, and by enabling local men to be trained in applying them.

The engineering firms of the first half of the nineteenth century were general shops which prided themselves on their self-sufficiency and their ability to turn their hands to a variety of products. In the north of Ireland, the best example was perhaps Victor Coates & Co. They started by making pots and pans, bleachers' equipment, and barkmills; their main activity became the making of steam engines and boilers, but they also built iron ships; they may have made cotton machinery, and although they did not make flax-spinning machinery they did make beetling engines, rub boards, and wash mills for finishing linen; they made equipment for many local industries including paper making, flour milling, distilling, and soap boiling; a large part of their business was structural work such as the building of cranes, bridges, and metal chimneys; they installed many water wheels, as well as power transmissions and mill gearing; they were also prepared to undertake repairs and jobbing work, and at one time acted as general ironfounders.

Other firms in Belfast, although not so versatile as Coates, undertook a variety of work until the 1860s and 1870s when specialisation became more pronounced. Exceptions were the general engineers and the provincial firms which concentrated on jobbing work rather than making products of their own design. The need for specialisation was dictated by specialisation in Britain, the larger scale of production, the increasing cost of machine tools, and the greater technical complexity of the industry which prevented any one firm being expert except in a continually narrowing field.

The increase in the scale of operations, combined with increasing competition and the fall in profit levels after the 1870s, led to amalgamations and other forms of combination in Britain, and to a much greater extent in America and Germany. In the north of Ireland, Mackies absorbed George Horner's textile machine-making business, and MacIlwaine & MacColl's shipyard was acquired by Workman Clark, but only one local engineering firm joined in a 'combine', the merger in 1900 of the Falls Foundry with two Leeds textile machinery firms to form Fairbairn Lawson Combe Barbour Ltd. Particularly when Lord Pirrie and his successor Lord Kylsant were chairmen, Harland & Wolff had extensive financial interests in shipping companies and steelmaking firms. The company also acquired a shareholding in the Belfast aircraft industry, but has not followed the example of other shipbuilders by joining a group of shipbuilding firms. In most branches of the industry, there were too few firms engaged in similar types of engineering in the north of Ireland to make mergers or other forms of combination worth while.

In recent years, the local industry has acquired links with large international organisations, not by their taking over existing Northern Ireland firms, but by establishing subsidiary companies in the province.

Technical Organisation

The making of steam engines was a job for specialists from the beginning; other forms of machinery were developed and improved by the users rather than the makers, until well into the second half of the nineteenth century. The machine makers had difficulty enough in mastering the technique of ironfounding and in making effective use of the new machine tools, without also becoming experts in the production of textiles or other goods. It was not until the 1860s, for example, that the engineering firms began to advance the design of textile machinery rapidly, and even later many important developments resulted from the work of men in the linen industry. Sir Samuel Davidson was a tea planter, not an owner of an engineering works, when he developed his original tea machinery.

While the engineering firms have taken the initiative in the design of new equipment, close technical co-operation with customers has remained an important characteristic. Research and design facilities in the industry generally were not well developed before 1914, but while the small firms continued to depend on customers for designs, the larger firms gradually improved their design departments, and after the second world war some firms, particularly Short Brothers & Harland, undertook research as well as design work. Research for industry was also undertaken by the Department of Industrial & Forensic Science, and by the Queen's University of Belfast, but most of the new engineering firms established since the 1950s continued to have their research and development work carried out at their parent establishments in Britain, America, or Europe.

There was no indication of any lack of inventive ability in the north of Ireland; patents were registered for almost every type of machinery made in the area and their number was substantial in the fields of marine engineering, textile machinery, and ventilating plant. As elsewhere, engineering firms usually started by imitating what was already being made because their owners were trained in existing firms; only a minority anywhere showed unusual skill in improving the existing level of technology. It was, however, to the few brilliant innovators such as Rider, Harland, Combe, and Davidson that the industry in the north of Ireland owed its development in the nineteenth century from a small group supplying the local market to a major employer of labour competing successfully in the world market.

The success of the industry in the twentieth century has continued to be based on good design rather than cheap materials or mass-production techniques. Firms in the north of Ireland have made better machinery for particular purposes than their competitors; they have not relied on making standard equipment more cheaply or more quickly.

If willingness to look for information and apply it is one of the characteristics of technically progressive firms, it must be admitted that most engineering firms in the north of Ireland have at least one claim to be progressive. Since the nineteenth century, new machine tools and processes have been quickly adopted and a close watch kept on the activities of competitors. Local engineers have generally been well informed on technical developments, and if there have been complaints in recent years that new ideas have not been put into practice quickly enough, this is a criticism which can be applied to industry generally and not only in the north of Ireland.

Commercial Organisation

In the nineteenth century the organisation and credit facilities necessary to supply the market with consumer goods told in favour of British producers in the Irish market. At that time most engineering firms in the north of Ireland sold capital equipment direct to their customers, and so required relatively simple marketing arrangements. In the case of ships or textile machinery, this meant negotiating at a high level and demanded an intimate knowledge of the product and its applications; it was a task which the partners in the firm could seldom delegate to their subordinates.

One of the most formidable salesmen from the north of Ireland was Lord Pirrie of Harland & Wolff, who travelled extensively in the ships built by his firm, noting what passengers wanted and the facilities available at the ports; he was frequently able to show shipowners opportunities for profitable investment in new ships, and to convince them that only Harland & Wolff could build the type of ships they needed.

The textile machinery makers used similar selling methods, attempting to show their customers how they could make money rather than being content with selling standard machinery. Close contact with a limited number of possible customers helped to build up goodwill for engineering firms in the north of Ireland, but no other local firms had such close relations with their customers as Harland & Wolff had with the White Star Line.

From the beginning, there was no formal contract for each ship; Harland & Wolff did not submit prices for ships but built them on a time and materials basis, and the owners did not lay down specifications; Harland & Wolff saved the trouble and expense of drawing up tenders and were assured of a percentage profit, while the White Star Line in return obtained a series of ships each of which was in its time first class for its purpose. This arrangement was based originally on the family relationship between G. W. Wolff and G. C. Schwabe of the White Star Line; it was continued and extended to other customers only because it was satisfactory in practice to both parties.

As practically no two firms in the local engineering industry made the same type of product, each had to develop its own marketing methods and sources of information, with the help of Chambers of Commerce and Government departments. In the 1880s and 1890s, the shipbuilders and marine engineers used the services of the Belfast employers' association to obtain information about trade in other centres. In 1884, for instance, they sent their secretary to sail up and down the Clyde, noting the number of vessels being built and the vacant slipways, and he arranged for a correspondent on the Clyde to write four letters a year giving details on the state of trade.

By the end of the nineteenth century, the textile machinery makers and the other large engineering firms had appointed agents or set up branch offices in the countries where they expected to be able to sell their products. In some cases depots and erection departments were also necessary, and since the second world war some firms have set up branch factories overseas; Davidson & Co, for example, has manufacturing facilities in Africa, Australia, and India.

Some local firms, such as Musgraves, had considerable success at the international industrial exhibitions in the second half of the nineteenth century, which were gathering places for engineers and potential customers where the latest developments were examined and discussed. The smaller firms, however, could not afford to have one of their principals engaged full time in selling, and had to rely on issuing catalogues and advertising in the technical press. Since the shipbuilders, textile machinery makers and other specialist firms were able to gain a foothold in the world market and retain their position, their selling methods must have been effective, but there was no common pattern of marketing. The influx of new firms since the 1950s has further complicated the position, since in most cases their sales organisations are located at the head office and not at the factory in Northern Ireland. The limited local market meant that the larger engineering firms in the north of Ireland have had to be vitally concerned with exports and interested in marketing as much as in production. They have had to make what they could sell, and not, like many firms in the industry elsewhere, be content to sell what they happened to be able to produce.

Management

The entrepreneur in the nineteenth century was no passive agent; he introduced new techniques of production, new methods of organisation and of managing labour, and kept in touch with developments in the market. It was not an easy matter to train young men for key posts in industry, and most businessmen owed their success to natural ability, rather than to systematic training. There was no certainty that the second and third generations in family firms would possess the qualities of the founder of the firm, and in many cases there was no member of the family to carry on the business.

Some firms closed on the death of the original owners, for instance the MacAdam brothers' Soho Foundry in Belfast, but in other cases younger men from the family or outside it were trained to carry on and expand the business when the founders retired from active participation in management. The best example is perhaps that of Harland & Wolff: W. J. Pirrie and Walter H. Wilson were able to carry on when Harland, and later Wolff, devoted their time to politics, nor was the expansion halted when the original partners died; even after Pirrie's death the management of the firm was carried on with equal vigour. A similar continuation of an expansionist policy was maintained in the family firm of James Mackie & Sons. It was mostly the smaller firms which suffered from breaks in the management succession, because there were few opportunities to attract ambitious men from outside, and no systematic policy of training within the firm.

The upper classes in Ireland were often said to be contemptuous of trade and industry; at the end of the eighteenth century, according to Arthur Young, the country gentlemen 'might be poor until doomsday but they were too proud to enter trade or manufacture, and Trinity College, Dublin, swarmed with lads who ought to be educated to the loom or the counting house'.[16] Even in 1896 the Recess Committee felt that to the middle and upper classes in Ireland there were still only three professions—the law, medicine, and the church.[17] In Belfast it was recognised by the middle of the nineteenth century that 'men were wanted in the more lucrative and perhaps equally learned employments concerned with the working of iron, the management of railways and kindred businesses' for which the town tended to import labour; in the foundries 'the best situations were frequently held by Scotch and English people'.[18] Up to 1900, however, little progress was made in evolving formal courses to supplement practical training on the job.

The courses in engineering at Queen's College, Belfast, were confined to civil engineering from 1849 until 1912, when courses in mechanical and electrical engineering were introduced, making use of the staff and facilities of the Belfast College of Technology. Even the facilities for the study of civil engineering in nineteenth-century Belfast were far from adequate. In his presidential address to the engineering section of the British Association meeting at Belfast in 1902, Professor John Perry, who had served his apprenticeship at the Lagan Foundry, said that when he entered Queen's College 'there was never on earth a college so poorly equipped for a course of engineering study' and the situation was redeemed only by the personality of the professor—James Thomson, elder brother of Lord Kelvin.[19] The new Belfast College of Technology was designed in the light of advances in technological education in Britain and on the Continent, and when it came into use in the first decade of the twentieth century was one of the best-equipped institutions of its kind in the United Kingdom. Close co-operation between the University and College in the provision of courses in mechanical and electrical engineering benefited both bodies; University students had courses made available which would probably not have been provided for them alone, while the College students had the services of highly qualified staff and well-equipped laboratories whose provision could not have been justified but for the presence of the University classes.

After the second world war, it became clear that a considerable expansion in the facilities for higher engineering education was required, and the Northern Ireland Government agreed to provide a new building to be used for University and College teaching and research in mechanical engineering, electrical engineering, and engineering mathematics. The Ashby Institute, which was opened in 1965, was again one of the best-equipped buildings of its kind in the United Kingdom, but it soon became obvious that it could not for long continue to provide adequate facilities for University and College courses, both of which were expanding. On the recommendation of the Lockwood Committee it was decided that non-University work should be transferred to a new Regional College of Technology, which will be completed at Jordanstown near Belfast early in the 1970s and will form part of the proposed Ulster College.

There was considerable interest in commercial education in nineteenth-century Belfast. Most of the boys who went to the Academical Institution in the first half of the century were the sons of businessmen, and young men in business commonly attended the Institution for an hour or two in the day; a number of men advanced themselves by part-time study, for example a brassfounder who became a Presbyterian minister, but it would probably have been considered a step in the wrong direction had a minister become a brassfounder. In 1860 the Belfast Chamber of Commerce agreed to support a scheme for 'extending to young men intended for mercantile pursuits the educational advantages of the Queen's College at Belfast' and also 'recommended the bankers, manufacturers, and merchants of Belfast and neighbourhood to lend support by giving preference to holders of the proposed college certificate or by shortening their terms of apprenticeship'. The course was intended mainly for 'the sons of gentlemen', but nothing came of it and there is no indication that anyone took the certificate. The matter was raised again by the College in 1874, without result; probably because those who would have benefited could attend only in the evenings, while the academic staff as a whole were unwilling to undertake regular evening teaching.

In 1901, the Chamber of Commerce set up a special committee on commercial education, which recommended the establishment of a school of commerce at Queen's College, Belfast, and the Chamber did not let the matter drop until a Faculty of Commerce was formed in 1910 at what had by then become the Queen's University of Belfast.[20] The depressions of the 1920s and 1930s restrained the expansion of commercial education, but from the 1950s additional courses were provided at both technical college and university level in commercial subjects and management studies. In the 1960s, the Northern Ireland Government encouraged the spread of new techniques of management by giving financial assistance to those attending appropriate courses and by paying grants to firms making use of the services of industrial consultants.

The Role of Enterprise

Enterprise was the key to progress in the north of Ireland, where there were no adequate supplies of raw materials, and at the beginning of the nineteenth century little skilled labour, where the local market was limited, and there were few profitable opportunities for the investment of capital. The key role of enterprise can be seen clearly in the case of the growth of shipbuilding at Belfast, and Sir Samuel Davidson's development of tea machinery, but in all cases it was the critical factor. Local engineering firms depended for their success on creating new products or on making better machinery for particular purposes than their competitors, rather than on competing with firms elsewhere in making less specialised equipment more cheaply or in offering earlier delivery dates; this policy minimised the effects of the economic difficulties under which they operated.

The problem is not to understand why industrial growth in the north of Ireland lagged behind that in Britain, but to explain why so much progress has been made in an area with so many economic disadvantages compared with Britain.

In the last analysis, the capacity to create wealth and employment resides in the people of a region and consists in brain power, enterprise, and inventiveness. In the English midlands, skill and enterprise exploited natural resources and remained the region's most valuable asset as resources fell short of the needs of local industry. In the engineering industry of the north of Ireland enterprise, maintained by periodic infusions of new blood from outside the province, imported skills, mobilised capital, found overseas markets, and more than balanced the lack of local resources.

Notes and References

CHAPTER TWO

1 Hall, Mr & Mrs S. C., *Ireland: its scenery, character etc*, III, 1843, p 154.
2 Rural Industries Development Committee, *Report on the farriery trade in Northern Ireland*, Belfast, 1966. There were probably another 4,000 horses used for pleasure.
3 Trimble, W. C., *History of Enniskillen*, III, Enniskillen, 1921, p 1035.
4 Olley & Co Ltd, *Commercial Ulster and the Home Rule movement*, Belfast, 1893, p 18.
5 Clark, G. (ed), *Industries of Ulster*, Belfast, 1882, p 21.
6 Johnston, T., *History of the working classes in Scotland*, 2nd edn, Glasgow, 1929, p 371.
7 Clapham, Sir John, *Economic history of modern Britain*, I, Cambridge, 1926, p 151.
8 Coe, Susan, *Irish clocks*, unpublished thesis, Belfast College of Art, 1960. The deal cases were subject to attack by woodworm and many have perished. The expensive clocks made in the north of Ireland have stood the test of time rather better, being made of longer lasting materials and receiving greater care from more affluent owners.

CHAPTER THREE

1 *Belfast News-Letter*, 8 July 1760, 8 January 1798.
2 Westropp, M. S. D., *Irish glass*, 1920, pp 99–105.
3 *Belfast News-Letter*, 18 June 1799, 6 March 1801, 23 March 1802.
4 *Belfast News-Letter*, 26 March 1811; Dubourdieu, Rev J., *Statistical survey of the county of Antrim*, Dublin, 1812, p 422.
5 Young, A., *Annals of agriculture*, III, 1785, p 393.
6 Most of the information about foundries has been obtained from the Belfast and provincial directories.
7 Wallace, T., *Essay on the manufactures of Ireland*, Dublin, 1798, p 230.
8 Wynne, R. W., *Business directory of Belfast and principal towns in the province of Ulster for 1865–66*, Belfast, 1865, adverts p 77.
9 O'Neill, H., 'Iron tombstones and the Pembrokeshire Coal and Iron Company', *Journal of Industrial Archaeology*, Vol 2 No 4, December 1965.

CHAPTER FOUR

1 Clark, G. (ed), *Industries of Ulster*, Belfast, 1882, pp 11, 13; Gribbon, H. D., *The history of water power in Ulster*, unpublished PhD thesis, Queen's University, Belfast, 1967. The power station on the river Erne is outside the area covered in this study.
2 Green, E. R. R., *The industrial archaeology of county Down*, Belfast, 1963, pp 52–8.
3 *Irish Commons Journal*, 1787, Vol XII, App DXXXV.
4 Young, R. M. (ed), *Historical notices of old Belfast*, Belfast, 1896, p 282; Young, R. M., *Belfast and the province of Ulster in the twentieth century*, Belfast, 1909, p 125.
5 Dubourdieu, Rev J., *Statistical survey of county Antrim*, Dublin, 1812, p 405; *Second report of the commissioners appointed to consider and recommend a general system of railways for Ireland, 1838*, App B, No 38, pp 112–13.
6 McCall, H., *Ireland and her staple manufactures*, 3rd edn, Belfast, 1870, p 482.
7 Patent specifications, 1805 No 2835, 1820 No 4490.
8 Dubourdieu, Rev J., *Statistical survey of county Antrim*, Dublin, 1812, p 421; Atkinson, A., *Ireland exhibited to England*, II, 1823, p 58; Martin, R. M., *Ireland before and after the union with Great Britain*, 3rd edn, 1848, p 64.
9 *Belfast News-Letter*, 1 January 1900; *Irish industrial exhibition—World's Fair, St Louis 1904*, Dublin, 1904.
10 Cressy, E., *A hundred years of mechanical engineering*, 1937, p 74.
11 Patent specifications, 1877 No 2013, 1883 No 649, 1894 No 9981.

CHAPTER FIVE

1 Monaghan, J. J., 'The rise and fall of the Belfast cotton industry', *Irish Historical Studies*, Vol 3, 1942, pp 1–8.
2 *Irish Commons Journal*, 1783, Vol XI, p 58.
3 *Irish Commons Journal*, 1783, Vol XI, p 55.
4 *Belfast News-Letter*, 22 September 1820.
5 Green, E. R. R., *The Lagan valley 1800–1850*, 1949, pp 99, 101, 110.
6 For an account of the Irish linen industry see: Gill, C., *The rise of the Irish linen industry*, Oxford, 1925; Green, E. R. R., *The Lagan valley 1800–1850*, 1949, pp 57–94.
7 *Industries of Ireland, Part 1, Belfast and the north*, 1891, p 127.
8 Marshall, L. C., *Practical flax spinner*, 1885, p 23.
9 Green, E. R. R., op cit, pp 82, 115–16.
10 Green, E. R. R., op cit, pp 112–13; Benn, G., *History of the town of Belfast*, II, 1880, p 132.

N

11 *Report from the select committee on the linen trade of Ireland, 1825*, pp 61–70.
12 *Belfast News-Letter*, 24 March 1812.
13 *Report from the select committee on the linen trade of Ireland, 1825*, p 47.
14 Horner, J., *The dawn of flax-spinning machinery*, Manchester, 1910, p 3; Horner, J., *The linen trade of Europe during the spinning-wheel period*, Belfast, 1920, p 263.
15 There are wide variations in the numbers of spindles given by different authorities. The most reliable figures seem to be those given in the annual reports of the Flax Supply Association.
16 Clapham, Sir John, *Economic history of modern Britain*, II, Cambridge, 1932, pp 85, 514.
17 Dickson, J. H., *A series of letters on the improved mode in the cultivation and management of flax*, 1846, p 99.
18 Maguire, J. F., *The industrial movement in Ireland*, Cork, 1853, p 178.
19 Charley, W. T., *Flax and its products in Ireland*, 1862, p 83.
20 Flax Supply Association, *Ninth report for year ended 31st December, 1875*, Belfast, 1876, p 44.
21 Belfast Naturalists' Field Club, *Guide to Belfast and the adjacent counties*, Belfast, 1874, pp 291–2.
22 Crawford, Sir William, *Irish linen and some features of its production*, Belfast, 1910, p 21.
23 Green, E. R. R., op cit, p 118.
24 Rigby, T., *Illustrated summer tour in the north of Ireland*, Altrincham, 1891, p 13.
25 Charley, W. T., op cit, p 88.
26 McCall, H., *Ireland and her staple manufactures*, 3rd edn, Belfast, 1870, pp 472–5.
27 Patent specification, 1879 No 4767.

CHAPTER SIX

1 Wilson, W. H., 'Recent advances in mechanical science', *Proceedings of the Belfast Natural History and Philosophical Society*, 1891–2, pp 148–50.
2 Rebbeck, D., 'The Belfast shipyards 1791–1947', *Belfast Association of Engineers*, Presidential address, 1947, pp 7–8. Doubt is cast on whether Coates built the engines of the *Belfast*, and whether the engines of the *Waterloo* were made in Cork, by Joshua Field's diary for 1821. 'Joshua Field's diary of a tour in 1821 through the provinces', *Transactions of the Newcomen Society*, Vol XIII, 1932–3, pp 34, 38, 48.
3 Anderson, E. B., *Sailing ships of Ireland*, Dublin, 1951, pp 235, 236.
4 *Belfast People's Magazine*, 3 April 1847.
5 Graham, G. S., 'The ascendancy of the sailing ship', *Economic History Review*, 2nd series, Vol 9, No 1, 1956, pp 76, 81, 87; Fayle, C. E., *Short history of the world's shipping industry*, 1933, pp 239, 240.

6 Anderson, E. B., op cit, pp 222–7, 246–53, 271–4.
7 Harland, E. J., 'Shipbuilding in Belfast', in Smiles, S., *Men of invention and industry*, 1884, pp 306–9.
8 Oldham, W. J., *The Ismay Line*, Liverpool, 1961, p 33.
9 Gibbs, C. R. V., *Passenger liners of the western ocean*, 1952, p 185.
10 For an illustrated account of Harland & Wolff's ships see: Dunn, L., *Famous liners of the past: Belfast built*, 1964.
11 Pounder, C. C., 'Some notable Belfast-built engines', *Proceedings of the Belfast Association of Engineers*, 1948, pp 12–21.
12 Owen, D. J., *History of Belfast*, Belfast, 1921, pp 304, 305; *Industries of Ireland, Part 1, Belfast and the north. 1891*, p 71.
13 For an illustrated account of Workman Clark ships see: Dunn, L., *Famous liners of the past: Belfast built*, 1964; Workman Clark (1928) Ltd, *Shipbuilding at Belfast 1880–1933*, 1934.
14 Jefferson, H., *Viscount Pirrie of Belfast*, Belfast, 1947, p 201.
15 Anderson, R., *White Star*, Prescot, 1964, pp 168, 169.
16 Oldham, C. H., 'The history of Belfast shipbuilding', *Proceedings of the Statistical and Social Inquiry Society of Ireland*, Vol 12, 1911, pp 421, 426.
17 *Report of the shipbuilding inquiry committee*, Cmnd 2937, 1966, pp 65–7.

CHAPTER SEVEN

1 *Northern Whig*, 7 January 1836.
2 Silbertson, A., 'The motor industry', in Burn, D. (ed), *The structure of British industry*, Cambridge, 1958, Vol 2, p 1.
3 *Belfast News-Letter*, 1 January 1914.
4 Illustrated in *Cooper's Vehicle Journal*, January 1916.
5 Maxcy, C. & Silbertson, A., *The motor industry*, 1956, p 79.
6 Patterson, E. M., *The Great Northern Railway of Ireland*, Lingfield, 1962, p 91.
7 Patterson, E. M., *The Great Northern Railway of Ireland*, Lingfield, 1962, pp 89, 90, App 4.
8 Patterson, E. M., *The Belfast & County Down Railway*, Lingfield, 1958, p 22.
9 Patterson, E. M., *The Ballymena lines*, Newton Abbot, 1968, p 123, plates 32, 33.
10 Clements, R. N., 'Locomotive building in Ireland', *Journal of the Irish Railway Record Society*, 5 December 1946.
11 Fayle, H., 'Belfast tramways', *Modern Tramway*, July 1940, p 78.
12 Camlin, E., in *Belfast Telegraph*, 10 August 1967; *Shorts Quarterly Review*, Vol 3, No 9, 1964, pp 14–17.
13 *Shorts Quarterly Review*, Vol 3, No 8, 1964, pp 14–17; Lewis, P., 'Lilian Bland and the Mayfly', *Flight International*, 23 January 1964, pp 140, 141.
14 Barnes, C. H., *Shorts aircraft since 1900*, 1967, p 488.

15 A well-illustrated account of Shorts and their aircraft is given in Barnes, C. H., *Shorts aircraft since 1900*, 1967.

CHAPTER EIGHT

1 *Industries of Ireland, Part 1, Belfast and the north*, 1891, p 114.
2 Clark, G. (ed), *Industries of Ulster*, Belfast, 1882, p 21.
3 *Modern Ireland—men of the period—selected from centres of commerce and industry*, 1899, p 138. Stable fittings appear to have been made up to the middle of the 1930s.
4 Wymer, N., *Harry Ferguson*, 1961, pp 24, 28, 38, 41, 42, 47, 67.
5 Murphy, J. N., *Ireland—industrial, political and social*, 1870, p 200.
6 *Belfast News-Letter*, 28 March 1800.
7 MaGuire, E. D., 'The birth and growth of an industry', *Belfast Association of Engineers*, Presidential address, 1954.
8 Clark, G., op cit, p 28. Tobacco spinning machines were similar to rope-making machines.
9 *Industries of Ireland*, p 96.
10 Smith, F. W., *Irish Textile Journal Directory for 1887*, Belfast, 1887, p xxx.
11 *Industries of Ireland*, p 23.
12 MaGuire, E. D., op cit.
13 Lewis, S., *Topographical dictionary of Ireland*, 2nd edn, 1846, Vol 1, p 137.
14 Clark, G., op cit, p 19.
15 Belfast Chamber of Commerce, *Commercial year book*, Belfast, 1909, p 220.

CHAPTER NINE

1 Lynch, P. & Vaizey, J., *Guiness's brewery in the Irish economy 1759–1876*, Cambridge, 1960, pp 9, 16.
2 Wallace, T., *Essay on the manufactures of Ireland*, Dublin, 1798, pp 224, 225.
3 *Report of the departmental committee of inquiry into the operation of the Agriculture and Technical Instruction (Ireland) Act, 1899*, Minority report by W. L. Micks, Cd 3575, 1907, p 138.
4 *Irish Industrial Magazine*, Vol 1, 1866, pp 397, 398.
5 Black, R. D. C., *Economic thought and the Irish question*, Cambridge, 1960, p 248.
6 Preston, W., 'Essay on the natural advantages of Ireland', *Transactions of the Royal Irish Academy*, Vol IX, 1803, pp 261–2 (written in 1786).
7 Oldham, C. H., 'The economics of industrial revival in Ireland', *Journal of the Statistical and Social Inquiry Society of Ireland*, Vol XII, 1908, p 184.
8 *Report of the Census of Production of Northern Ireland, 1965*, Belfast, 1967, p 8.
9 Maguire, J. F., *The industrial movement in Ireland*, Cork, 1853, p 178.

10 Clapham, Sir John, *Economic history of modern Britain*, Vol 1, Cambridge, 1926, p 448.
11 Clapham, op cit, Vol 2, p 117.
12 Isles, K. S. & Cuthbert, N., *Economic survey of Northern Ireland*, Belfast, 1957, p 117.
13 *Report of the Census of Production of Northern Ireland, 1963*, Vol 3, p 2.
14 Herring, I. C., 'Ulster roads on the eve of the railway age', *Irish Historical Studies*, Vol 2, No 6, 1940, p 187.
15 Hall, Mr & Mrs S. C., *Ireland: its scenery, character etc*, Vol 1, 1841, p 1.
16 Mulholland, J., 'Concluding address at Belfast meeting, 1867', *Transactions of the National Association for the Promotion of Social Science*, 1867, p 16.
17 Oldham, op cit, p 182.

CHAPTER TEN

1 Fraser, R., *Gleanings in Ireland, particularly respecting its agriculture, mines and fisheries*, 1802, p 4.
2 Crory, W. G., *Treatise on industrial resources (still neglected) in Ireland*, Dublin, 1860, p 11.
3 Coyne, W. P., *Ireland industrial and agricultural*, Dublin, 1901, p 27.
4 Jones, E., *Social geography of Belfast*, 1960, p 41.
5 Scrivenor, H., *History of the iron trade*, 2nd edn, 1854, p 60.
6 Andrews, J. H., 'Notes on the historical geography of the Irish iron industry', *Irish Geography*, Vol 3, No 3, 1956; McCracken, Eileen, 'Charcoal-burning ironworks in seventeenth and eighteenth century Ireland', *Ulster Journal of Archaeology*, 3rd series, Vol 20, 1957; McCracken, Eileen, 'Supplementary list of Irish charcoal-burning ironworks', *Ulster Journal of Archaeology*, 3rd series, Vol 28, 1965. The principal ironworks in the north were at: Lagan Valley—Ardoyne, Old Forge, New Forge, Stranmillis, Lambeg, Carrickfergus, Whitehouse. North and west of Lough Neagh—Toome, Randalstown, Kilrea, Salterstown, Lissan, Draperstown, Maghera, Castledawson, Magherafelt, Kirlish. Lough Erne— Garrison, Clonelly, Drumcro, Castlecaldwell.
7 Schubert, H. R., *History of the British iron and steel industry*, 1957, p 146.
8 Benn, G., *History of the town of Belfast*, Vol 1, 1877, pp 319, 334.
9 Maguire, J. F., *The industrial movement in Ireland*, Cork, 1853, p 179. There is a detailed description of the Arigna ironworks in Fraser, R., *Gleanings in Ireland*, 1802, Appendix.
10 *Geological survey of Ireland*, explanatory memoir to accompany sheet 55, Dublin, 1885, p 29.
11 *Commission on the natural and industrial resources of Northern Ireland— report on mineral resources*, 1925, Cmd 43, pp 43, 44.
12 Pierson, J. G., *Great ship builders, or the rise of Harland & Wolff*, 1935, p 8.

13 *Report on the trade in imports and exports at Irish ports during the year ended 31st December, 1913*, 1914–16, Cd 7639, p 67.
14 Davies, G. L., 'The town and coalfield of Ballycastle', *Irish Geography*, Vol 3, No 4, 1957; Wilson, G. A., *The rise and decline of the Ballycastle coalfield 1770–1840*, unpublished MA thesis, Queen's University of Belfast, 1951.
15 Griffith, R., *Geological and mining survey of the coal districts of the counties of Tyrone and Antrim*, Dublin, 1829; Hutchison, W. R., *Tyrone precinct*, Belfast, 1951, pp 130–48; Fowler, A. & Robbie, J. A., *Geology of the country around Dungannon*, 2nd edn, Belfast, 1961.
16 *Irish Commons Journal*, 31 October 1751, 8 November 1751.
17 *Irish Commons Journal*, 1 November 1753, 8 November 1753.
18 *Belfast News-Letter*, 2 May 1755.
19 *Belfast News-Letter*, 10 February 1758. It seems unlikely that the works was reopened.
20 *Irish Industrial Magazine*, Vol 1, 1866, p 223.
21 Lewis, S., *Topographical dictionary of Ireland*, 2nd edn, 1846, Vol 1, p 634.
22 Kane, Sir Robert, *Industrial resources of Ireland*, Dublin, 1844, pp 57, 59, 60.
23 Wilson, A. B., 'Power and its transmission', *Proceedings of the Belfast Natural History and Philosophical Society*, 1887, p 35.
24 Isles, K. S. & Cuthbert, N., *Economic survey of Northern Ireland*, Belfast, 1957, p 145.

CHAPTER ELEVEN

1 *The Belfast meeting of the Trades Union Congress, 1893*, reprinted from the *Belfast News-Letter*, Belfast, 1893, p 31.
2 Handley, J. E., *The Irish in modern Scotland*, Cork, 1947, pp 95–118.
3 Kennedy, D., 'The Catholic church', in Moody, T. W. & Beckett, J. C. (ed), *Ulster since 1800*, 2nd series, 1957, p 178.
4 Gray, W., *Science and art in Belfast*, Belfast, 1904.
5 *Report of the Recess Committee on the establishment of a department of agriculture and industries for Ireland*, Dublin, 1896, p 90.
6 Dubourdieu, Rev J., *Statistical survey of the county of Antrim*, Dublin, 1812, p 341.
7 *Report of inquiry into the condition of the poorer classes in Ireland*, 1836, App c, p 6.
8 *Standard time rates of wages in the United Kingdom as at 1st October 1910*, 1910, Cd 5459, pp 34–6.
9 Jefferys, M. & J. B., 'The wages, hours and trade customs of the skilled engineer in 1861', *Economic History Review*, Vol 17, 1947, p 40.
10 *Report of the Joint Working Party on the Economy of Northern Ireland*, 1962, Cmd 446, p 65.

11 Fyrth, H. J. & Collins, H., *The foundry workers*, Manchester, 1959, p 72.
12 Connolly, J., *Labour in Ireland*, Dublin, 1944, p 274.
13 Belfast Engineers', Shipbuilders', Founders', and Machine Makers' Association, Indenture of Association, 1866.
14 The Ironfounders' Association of Ireland was formed early in the twentieth century. This was almost purely a price-fixing body, which from time to time issued printed price lists; it attracted into membership firms in the south as well as ironfoundries in the provincial towns in the north, which at that time showed no interest in joining the Belfast employers' association. There was also a Brassfounders' Association of Ireland with membership similar to that of the Ironfounders' Association. Little can be discovered about the activities of these associations as their records appear to be no longer available.
15 Jefferys, J. B., *The story of the engineers*, 1945, p 140.
16 *Belfast News-Letter*, 21 December 1897.

CHAPTER TWELVE

1 Jefferys, J. B., *The story of the engineers*, 1945, p 15.
2 Millin, S. S., *Sidelights on Belfast history*, Belfast, 1932, pp 71–9.
3 Hall, Mr & Mrs S. C., *Ireland: its scenery, character etc*, Vol 3, 1843, p 55.
4 McCulloch, J. R., *Dictionary of commerce*, 1832, p 39.
5 Kerr, A. W., *History of banking in Scotland*, 2nd edn, 1908, pp 55, 56, 330.
6 Wallace, T., *Essay on the manufactures of Ireland*, Dublin, 1798, pp 59, 60, 65.
7 *List of shareholders in the Ulster Railway Company*, Belfast, 1837.
8 *Report of the joint working party on the economy of Northern Ireland*, Cmd 446, 1962, p 10; Isles, K. S. & Cuthbert, N., *Economic survey of Northern Ireland*, Belfast, 1957, pp 173–98.
9 *Irish Industrial Magazine*, Vol 1, 1866, p 224.
10 Compare Isles & Cuthbert, op cit, p 348.
11 Law, D., 'Industrial movement and locational advantage', *Manchester School*, Vol 32, No 2, May 1964, p 151.
12 Blackwood, R. W. H., Manuscript pedigrees of Northern Ireland families, Vol 15, p 74, Linenhall Library, Belfast; *Belfast News-Letter*, 18 June 1799, 23 February 1802. By 1823 Coates was making starch for bleachers and he also owned a cotton mill.
13 *Belfast Co-operative Advocate*, No 2, March 1830, p 27.
14 Fyrth, H. J. & Collins, H., *The foundry workers*, Manchester, 1959, p 88.
15 Wilson, A., 'The shipbuilding industry in Belfast', *Proceedings of the Belfast Natural History and Philosophical Society*, 1915, p 11.
16 Young, A., *Tour in Ireland*, Vol 2, 2nd edn, 1780, p 343.
17 *Report of the recess committee on the establishment of a department of agriculture and industries for Ireland*, Dublin, 1896, p 88.

18 *Irish Industrial Magazine,* Vol 1, 1866, p 317.
19 British Association for the Advancement of Science, *Report of the Belfast meeting, 1902,* 1903, p 714.
20 Belfast Chamber of Commerce, *Report presented at meeting held on 16 January, 1860,* p 10; Moody, T. W. & Beckett, J. C., *Queen's, Belfast 1845–1949,* Vol 1, 1959, pp 93, 160.

Acknowledgments

THE author is indebted to all those associated with the engineering industry in the north of Ireland who answered his many queries or allowed him to consult records in their possession, but especially to Mr T. H. Kernohan, Director of the Engineering Employers' Northern Ireland Association and Mr J. Morrow, Irish Divisional Organiser of the Amalgamated Union of Engineering and Foundry Workers. A special debt of gratitude is owed to Professor K. H. Connell, Queen's University of Belfast, who supervised the author's researches into the history of the industry. Much valuable assistance has also been received from the staff of the Public Record Office of Northern Ireland, the Linenhall Library, Belfast, the Belfast City Library, the Library of the Queen's University of Belfast, the Ulster Museum, the Ulster Folk Museum, and the Transport Museum at Belfast.

Bibliography

THE following bibliography is restricted to published material directly relevant to the engineering industry in the north of Ireland. For background reading reference should be made to works on the history of Ireland, economic history, and the history of technology. Much valuable information is contained in British and Northern Ireland parliamentary papers, the census of population and census of production, exhibition catalogues, local directories, guide books and newspapers. There are important collections of books relating to the north of Ireland in the Linen Hall Library, Belfast, and the Belfast Central Library. Unpublished material essential for the study of local industry is contained in the Public Record Office of Northern Ireland, the records of the Engineering Employers' Northern Ireland Association and the trade unions in Northern Ireland, the Ulster Museum, the Ulster Folk Museum, and the Transport Museum in Belfast, and in theses in the Queen's University of Belfast,

General

Beckett, J. C., *The making of modern Ireland 1603–1923*, 1966.
Beckett, J. C. & Glasscock, R. E. (ed), *Belfast—the origin and growth of an industrial city*, 1967.
Benn, G., *History of the town of Belfast*, Belfast, 1823.
History of the town of Belfast, 2 vols, Belfast, 1877, 1880.
Black, R. D. C., *Economic thought and the Irish question 1817–1870*, Cambridge, 1960.
Blake, J. W., *Northern Ireland in the Second World War*, Belfast, 1956.
British Association for the Advancement of Science, *Belfast in its regional setting*, Belfast, 1952.
Chart, D. A., *An economic history of Ireland*, Dublin, 1920.
A history of Northern Ireland, Belfast, 1927.
Fullarton, A. & Co, *Parliamentary gazetteer of Ireland*, 3 vols, Dublin, 1844.
Green, E. R. R., *The Lagan valley 1800–1850*, 1949.
Hutchison, W. R., *Tyrone precinct*, Belfast, 1951.
Isles, K. S. & Cuthbert, N., *An economic survey of Northern Ireland*, Belfast, 1957.
Jones, E., *A social geography of Belfast*, 1960.
Lewis, S., *Topographical dictionary of Ireland*, 2nd edn, 1846.

Moody, T. W. & Beckett, J. C. (ed), *Ulster since 1800—a political and economic survey*, 1955.

Ulster since 1800—a social survey, 1957.

O'Brien, G., *The economic history of Ireland in the seventeenth century*, Dublin, 1919.

The economic history of Ireland in the eighteenth century, Dublin, 1918.

The economic history of Ireland from the Union to the Famine, 1921.

Owen, D. J., *Short history of the port of Belfast*, Belfast, 1917.

History of Belfast, Belfast, 1921.

Pilson, J. A., *History of the rise and progress of Belfast and annals of the county Antrim*, Belfast, 1846.

Report of the joint working party on the economy of Northern Ireland, Cmd 446, Belfast, 1962.

Ulster Year Book 1966–1968, Belfast, 1967.

Wilson, T. (ed), *Ulster under home rule*, Oxford, 1955.

Wilson, T., *Economic development in Northern Ireland, including the report of the economic consultant Professor Thomas Wilson*, Cmd 479, Belfast, 1965.

Industry

Anderson, R., *White Star*, Prescot, 1964.

Barbour, W. T., 'Falls Foundry Belfast 1848–1956', *Textile Quarterly*, Vol 6, Nos 3 & 4, 1956.

Barnes, C. H., *Shorts aircraft since 1900*, 1967.

Biographical Publishing Company, *Modern Ireland, men of the period, selected from centres of commerce and industry*, 1899.

Boate, G., *Ireland's naturall history*, 1652.

Burstall, A. F., *History of mechanical engineering*, 1963.

Charley, W., *Flax and its products in Ireland*, 1862.

Clark, G. (ed), *The industries of Ulster*, Belfast, 1882.

Coyne, W. P. (ed), *Ireland industrial and agricultural*, 2nd edn, Dublin, 1902.

Cressy, E., *A hundred years of mechanical engineering*, 1937.

Dunn, L., *Famous liners of the past: Belfast built*, 1964.

Dunsheath, P., *History of electrical engineering*, 1962.

Gill, C., *The rise of the Irish linen industry*, Oxford, 1925.

Green, E. R. R., *The industrial archaeology of county Down*, Belfast, 1963.

Gribbon, H. D., *The history of waterpower in Ulster*, in preparation.

Harland, E. J., 'Shipbuilding in Belfast', in Smiles, S., *Men of invention and industry*, 1884.

Historical Publishing Company, *Industries of Ireland, Part I, Belfast and the towns of the north*, 1891.

Report from the select committee on industries (Ireland), (288), 1884–5.

Jefferson, H., *Viscount Pirrie of Belfast*, Belfast, 1947.

Kane, Sir Robert, *The industrial resources of Ireland*, Dublin, 1844.

MaGuire, E. D., 'The birth and growth of an industry', *Proceedings of the Belfast Association of Engineers*, 1954.

Maguire, J. F., *The industrial movement in Ireland as illustrated by the national exhibition of 1852*, Cork, 1853.

McCall, H., *Ireland and her staple manufactures*, 3rd edn, Belfast, 1870.

Commission on the natural and industrial resources of Northern Ireland, report on the mineral resources of Northern Ireland, Cmd 43, Belfast, 1925.

Oldham, C. H., 'The history of Belfast shipbuilding', *Proceedings of the Statistical and Social Inquiry Society of Ireland*, 1911.

Oldham, W. J., *The Ismay Line*, Liverpool, 1961.

Pounder, C. C., 'Some notable Belfast-built engines', *Proceedings of the Belfast Association of Engineers*, 1948.

Preston, W., 'Essay on the natural advantages of Ireland, the manufactures to which they are adapted and the best means of improving those manufactures', *Transactions of the Royal Irish Academy*, Vol 9, 1803 (written 1796).

Rebbeck, D., 'The Belfast shipyards 1791–1947', *Proceedings of the Belfast Association of Engineers*, 1947.

Commission of inquiry into the resources and industries of Ireland, Dublin, 1921.

Schubert, H. R., *History of the British iron and steel industry, BC 450–AD 1775*, 1957.

Report of the shipbuilding inquiry committee, Cmnd 2937, 1966.

Sproule, J. (ed), *The Irish Industrial Exhibition of 1853*, Dublin, 1854.

Sullivan, W. K. (ed), *The Cork Industrial Exhibition of 1883*, Cork, 1886.

Wallace, T., *An essay on the manufactures of Ireland*, Dublin, 1798.

Wilson, A., 'The shipbuilding industry in Belfast', *Proceedings of the Belfast Natural History and Philosophical Society*, 1915.

Workman Clark (1928) Ltd, *Shipbuilding at Belfast 1880–1933*, 1934.

Wymer, N., *Harry Ferguson*, 1961.

Industrial Relations

Clarkson, J. D., *Labour and nationalism in Ireland*, New York, 1925.

Connolly, J., *Labour in Irish history*, Dublin, 1910.

   Labour in Ireland, Dublin, 1944.

Cummings, D. C., *A historical survey of the Boiler Makers and Iron and Steel Ship Builders Society from August 1834 to August 1904*, Newcastle-on-Tyne, 1905.

Engineering and Allied Employers' National Federation, *Thirty years of industrial conciliation*, 1927.

Fyrth, H. J. & Collins, H., *The foundry workers*, Manchester, 1959.

Jefferys, J. B., *The story of the engineers*, 1945.

Marsh, A., *Industrial relations in engineering*, Oxford, 1965.

Mortimer, J. E., *History of the Association of Engineering and Shipbuilding Draughtsmen*, 1960.
Mosses, W., *The history of the United Patternmakers' Association*, 1922.
Shadwell, A., *The engineering industry and the crisis of 1922*, 1922.
Stevens, W. C., *The story of the E.T.U.*, Bromley, 1952.

Index

Illustrations are indicated by bold type

222